MAKING WORDS SING

Exploring the sounds, silences and sensations of poetry

SAMANTHA BEARDON.

Highdene Publishing

November 2019

IBSN – 978-1-5272-5052-9

Acknowledgements

My thanks to the poets who I have worked with and learned so much from. Especially those kindred spirits in Rising Moon, my Facebook group who have bandied ideas, critiqued my work, mentored me and shared their awesome poetry with us.

Special thanks go to the poets who have allowed me to share their works in this book; they are all great poets and you can learn so much from reading their work.

Thanks go to all my Facebook students who have helped me think laterally about poetry.

I must also say a big thank you to my husband David and my friend Danielle for the proof reading.

An even bigger thank you for the formatting help and drawings from David.

Table of Contents

The Ethos of Poetry

Poetry is teased from emotions which should be recollected in tranquillity, before being drawn on the page distilled, considered and perfected. It is also emotion reflected and enhanced by sound; the lilt and swell of the cadence of song. Poetry often preserves the moment, a fleeting instant, an emotion that would be passed and be lost to memory. Poetry adds a sense of reason, rightness and logic. It builds on the memories and experiences of the reader to make them a partner; reading poetry is **not** a passive activity.

Most poetry tells a fraction of a story, sets out the parameters, and encourages the reader to experience life with the narrator and to people the poem with their own interpretations. Poetry is never static; each reader takes it and adds depth and interpretation to the story. It is written to evoke a reaction. It is not always the reaction the poet intended.

As poets we need the reader's involvement in our work; passive recipients do not engage fully. If we have a specific message, we need to ensure that we use imagery and context to ensure clarity whilst leaving space, 'dreaming room' for the reader to think, react and add their own dimension. To do this well, we need to understand and practice the skill set available to poets. These skills are highlighted in the following pages.

Poetry is in our DNA; it's there in the cadence of our speech, our everyday use of emphasis and metaphor. Poetry dates back some 4300 years. Written poetry is the most ancient record of human literature. The roots are likely to reach much further into the past, to a time when literacy had not yet evolved, and poems were passed down in oral traditions. The fact that poetry has accompanied humankind over such a long period suggests a strong grip on human beings and their emotions.

Poetry is as wide as the world. It portrays emotions in a way a reader may not dare, it can allow people who cannot or do not know how to express emotion to do so through imagery and ideas. It opens the flood gates of the imagination.

Poetry comes in a wide variety of forms, such as Free Verse, Couplet, Sonnet, Quatrain, Ballad, Haiku, Tanka, Villanelle, Blank Verse and many more. Several of these forms were written originally in languages other than in English but have been developed into English forms over the centuries. Form indicates the way words and sounds are patterned in the poetic structure and how that structure will sit on the page and deliver sound to affect meaning and emotion.

Everybody has poetry that speaks to them. As with art, food and fiction we all enjoy different things. Yet over time whilst new styles of poetry are developed and hold sway, the musicality, the rhythm of classical forms still holds a place in many hearts. Poetry in different guises has always accompanied humankind and each country has its own songs, poetry and poets.

The beauty and wonder of pictures and emotions distilled into a short poem can be breath-taking. This should be our aim as poets to be skilled enough to draw our readers into a place of wonder or a place of sorrow with conviction to immerse them in our world. Read this book to find tricks to make your poetry sing.

Poetic Choir

Whether you are a new writer of poetry or a more seasoned poet I hope this book will stimulate ideas to enable you to enhance your poetic voice.

Poetry is an art form; a broad genre that covers many forms and styles. What is good poetry? That of course is as subjective as the appreciation of paintings, music and books in general.

Personal taste will always play a significant role in what speaks to us, what captures our attention, tugs at our heart strings. A good poem will have certain characteristics for each of us personally such as something we stop and read more than once, that we find ourselves thinking about after the initial read, and something that gives us some sort of visceral reaction.

Generically the characteristics of a good poem are that it is:

Well written

Entertaining

Authentic

Interesting

Evocative

Poetry is painting pictures with words, making music with the sound of words, it is manipulating language to create magical imagery. Poetry can wow the reader, educate them, dovetail with their mood, move them, make them laugh or cry. To enable our poems to resonate with our readers we need to be highly skilled in poetic techniques.

What you write about is up to you. This book won't tell you that; you have to find your subjects and write. You may well find ideas here, but your personal interests and life experiences will populate your poems.

What I will try to do is improve your techniques and help you to think like a poet. The gift, the talent comes from inside you but the techniques to make your ideas shine and sing need practice, as with every skill we ever learn. Writing is more than just a magical gift; it is an art and artists of all types learn individual skills and techniques to further their craft.

It is so with poetry. A poem may or may not have a specific number of lines, rhyme scheme and/or metrical pattern, but it can still be labelled according to its form or style. Here are the three most common types of poems according to form:

11

Lyric Poetry: It is any poem with one speaker who expresses strong thoughts and feelings. A lyric poem is a private expression of emotion by an individual. The focus is on creating a mood or recalling a feeling. Lyric poetry is highly musical and can feature poetic devices like rhyme and meter. It tends to be a shorter poem than the narrative poem. Most poetry, especially contemporary poetry is lyric. Poems such as sonnets, odes and much free verse is lyric poetry.

Narrative Poetry: This is a poem that tells a story; its structure resembles the plot line, with the introduction of conflict, characters, rising action, climax and the denouement. It often combines poetic techniques such as alliteration. It tends to have a beginning, middle and end.

One type of narrative poem is the ballad, that was originally designed to be chanted or sung.

Descriptive Poem: This is a poem that describes the world that surrounds the speaker. The feelings the poet has are secondary to the description. Those feelings don't get in the way of the imagery. It uses elaborate imagery and adjectives. While emotional, it is more "outward-focused" than lyric poetry, which is more personal and introspective.

I am going to start by giving you a few good poems to get the poetical juices flowing, visit the tools you need in your poetic toolbox and suggest some exercises that could strengthen your overall poetic technique.

Remember it is very difficult to try to isolate poetic devices in this way – to separate out, for example, the effects of rhythm from rhyme. This doesn't mean that we shouldn't look for particular techniques at work in a poem, but we need to be aware that they will be interdependent, the recipe combines ingredients and the end product of the mingix is what will make a poem effective or not, because of the way such elements work together.

To unleash our creativity, we need to go beyond the conventional way we see the world and unlock our deepest passions, unleash all of our senses. I hope this book will enable you to begin that process.

What equipment do you need to be a poet?

An enquiring mind, imagination, a notebook, pencil and a good dictionary.

A burning desire to write.

Poetic voice

In poetry, the term 'voice' refers to the way in which a poet translates what's in their head to the outside world. Poetic voice is very simply the way that the poet writes. It is the choice of words, the order of words, the length of lines, the weight of stanzas, the length of poems. The way imagery is used, the choice of subjects, outlook, and everything else that goes into the writing of a poem.

A poet uses a voice for a poem and projects that voice to an audience. Frances Mayes suggests that poets develop specific voices to connect to the reader. 'The personal "I" voice, the public voice, the invisible voice.' *Frances Mayes. page139. The Discovery of Poetry. Harcourt. New York. 2001.*

The personal voice allows the reader to react to a direct personal expression or experience in the poem. This allows the reader to feel closer to the voice. The poet uses the public voice to represent a group of people in a common situation, they do this by forming a relationship with the reader by the utilising "we". The public voice conveys the writer's attitude to controversial, political, religious or sensitive subjects. It implies shared interest and experiences.

Poetic voice is rooted in the use and repetition of elements that make a poem recognisable as belonging to a poet. Those elements are syntax, grammar, form, sound and music, rhythm and diction. Plus of course the dash of magic the connection between the poet, the poem and the reader.

One of the things the new poet must do is develop their voice and experimenting with poetic tools and styles is part of that. Those of us who begin our poetry journey in love with rhyme don't lose that, but we come to appreciate we need to communicate through our poetry I different ways to fully engage a wider audience. Your poetic voice will develop grow and change as your poetic abilities change but there will always be characteristics of of your writing style that will be evident and signpost your writing.

Although, you will need to learn to change the essence of the voice projection when choosing how to approach a poem if you want to write convincingly. Some of the voices used by poets are the audible voice the one that carries the pitch tone and rhythm. The authoritative voice the one that makes the strong speech and has conviction of accuracy and honesty. The dramatic voice the performance voice like a character in a play. The distinctive signature voice of the poet when not projecting in tongues!

'The building blocks of poetry itself are elements of fiction – fable, "image", metaphor – all the material of the nonliteral. The components of verse are like parts of plans the materials are built into a structure. The study of rhetoric distinguishes between tropes, or figures of meaning such as metaphor and metonymy, and schemes or surface patterns of words. Poetry is a matter of trope, and verse, of scheme or design.'
Page 1. John Hollander. Rhyme's Reason. Yale University Press.

Reading Poetry like a poet

The principles of reading and thinking about poetry apply equally to readers as well as poets but here I want you to concentrate on the pieces as works of art, but more importantly as pieces of learning. Use these poems as templates, as resources for the use of poetic devices. Dissect them and look for the pieces that work well and reason out why. Where I illustrate poetic devices in the sections, come back to the poem and look at how it works in relation to the whole poem.

Look and think about the **title** of the piece.

What message has the title given you? What expectations does it give you? What does it tell you about the subject? Hold that thought and come back to the title after several read-throughs.

Read the poem all the way through more than **once**.

Read the poem **aloud**; it can be semi-aloud or mouthed quietly. Feel the sounds coming from the mouth, listen to it. Poetry has rhythm and musical qualities; hear them, feel them. Often the mood of the poem can be judged by the rhythm.

Is the poem talking about a specific issue, making a point, an argument, telling a story or describing something?

What does the poem look like on the page? How has the poet used line length and white space? Has the poem a look that draws you to read or pushes you away?

What are your initial feelings; the positive and the negative? You may change your mind later but it's good to crystallise initial thoughts.

What words has the poet used?

Look up any words you don't know. Underline or jot down any words that feel important. Look at the words at the end of lines this is a place of prime importance. Take note of the meanings and connotations of the words and any patterns.

Patterns in poetry are important. Look for repeat words or phrases, synonyms, repeat sounds, and the symmetry or otherwise of the lines and spaces.

Try to think why particular words were chosen from a whole range of words that might have said much the same? What did the poet mean by their choice of word?

What message is the poet giving?

Who is speaking, man or woman? Which tense is being used?

Can you tell the mood of the narrator?

How is the poem organized? How is it divided up? Are there individual verses or numbered sections or no divisions? What does each section or stanza discuss? How are the sections or stanzas related to each other?

If there are no formal divisions, try breaking down the poem line by line. The poet's thinking process may not be logical, but there is probably an emotional link between ideas.

A very controlled structure may tell you a lot about the poet's attitude toward the subject. Is it a very formal topic? Is the poet trying to get a grip on something chaotic? A freer poetic form with less structure may also clue you in to the poets thinking.

Now that you have taken time to really know the poem, reread it and consider the whole.

What in your opinion is the poet trying to say? How forcefully does he or she say it and with what feeling?

Which lines bring out the meaning of the poem? Does the poet gradually lead up to the meaning or does he or she state it right at the beginning?

What are the last lines saying? They often emphasize or change the meaning of the poem. Is this so in the poem that you are reading?

Is it well crafted? Has the poet taken care with word choice? Punctuation? Grammar? Sound? Which are the lines that bring meaning to the message for you?

Has the poet told you the message, or has the poet made you see the images and feel the emotions along with the narrator? Is it something you would read again?

Was there a surprise within the poem? Did you learn something new? Or did it resonate with your ideas or feelings.

What have you learnt from the structure of the poem?

Read the poem again. Mark it up; write in the margins; react to it; get involved with it. Circle important, striking, or repeated words. Draw lines to connect related ideas. Mark difficult or confusing words, lines, and passages.

Now read the piece again out loud feeling it, almost taste it and listen to the sounds, chimes and cadences.

Now you are fully acquainted with the piece what do you think?

Why should Poets Read Poetry?

To write poetry it is important to read poetry of all genres. Whilst most of us can pick up a pen and instinctively write verse often with the primeval rhyme or beat of childhood rhymes and rhythms, there is so much more to the exquisite piece that draws you back time after time. The poet will have used various strategies to hone the poem to perfection. In order to understand the mechanism, we need to read and think about what makes the poem we are reading work as a poem.

Like with every art form some pieces will speak to us more than others, some pieces will annoy us, some frustrate us, some will send us on an emotional high. It is not enough to just write we have to understand the nuances of our craft and reading good poetry is a key to writing better poetry.

Let's Read some poetry

Music at Dusk by D.B. Hall

Autumn dusk can be so seductive
crisply sneaking in
unawares of the clock's pointy hands
erasing the day's heat.

Over-worked people emerge
from their social media slumber
stretching reclinered limbs
to the tune of rice krispies
catching breaths with forgotten lungs
eyes adjusting from apple screens.

Music with an easy-going vibe
teases out the last of the tangerine hues
slowly enticing the blues even before
the drummer begins to drum
or the guitar man starts to strum.

Bodies anchored by gravity of excess
bare feet caressed by fresh cut grass
automatically swaying
to an ancient beat
relaxing tense muscles
under the sweet notes of a sax
laughing souls
move on into the neon shadows
of a Corona night.

Remembering that seductive phase
separate from this disparate dusk
now a different melody plays;
a peaceful rhythm
resonating in the soul's marrow
under the sliver
of this slower rising moon.

Dying leaves fluttering to their siblings
accompanied by the soulful dirge
of crooning tree frogs
and serenading crickets;
a raspy coyote joins the unseen choir
in their melodious rhapsody
protesting the crisp nip of the air.

When darkness's blanket is complete
and silence sneaks in
slowly after a fading finale
time becomes so still.

The sound of Poplar and Pine
crackling in the fire
is a captivating tune
nice and low in the background
of a dance, danced ever so slow.

And without a word
fireflies flutter
into the trusting shadows
of a Carolina night.

Silence of the Birds by Samantha Beardon

Figures in a watercolour
suffused in cool misty washed out light
standing stark against the bare horizon
small dark images between shoreline
and the immense pearlescent sky.
Look closer
footprints along the edge of the wet mudflat
as the water recedes slinking away
like a cat in the grass
a cloud of black and white suddenly expelled
into the sky circling -returning
dark smudges with
white highlights from the emerging sun
oyster catchers swift and silent
in their awesome dance.
Press a button to add a soundtrack
the gentle rustling of the grass the slap
flap of jackets moving in the breeze
overlaid by the boom boom of the Bittern.
Figure in a watercolour
suffused in cold misty light
standing stark against steel grey sky
Caught betwixt sky and shoreline
A single grey heron
flys across the sky
The shoreline appears
as the sea recedes like
a cat slinking in the grass
No bird calls today as I make
my solitary way to the beach.

Scar Tissue by Susannah Bailey

You're seeking forgiveness
I cannot begin
To peel back the layers
Of you under my skin
Your usual mirror
Reflects your disguise
The sins of omission
Still add up to lies
Your needle-sharp tongue
Slips straight through the scars
If you still want to hurt
You'll have to push hard
This is not hope
Which makes my heart quicken
It's scar tissue simply
Beginning to thicken
You're seeking forgiveness
It lies beyond me
My senses are vaulted
And you snapped the key
The secrets of silence
Are scattered and broken
Those poisonous lips
Have already spoken
Forgiveness you're seeking
Should never be needed
Love doesn't tally

The points we've conceded
A crack in the structure
Is steadily leaking
Along with redemption
You claim to be seeking
You tug at a thought
It's not what you said
You pull it taut and I'm
cutting the thread.

Counter song by K Ryan

If the final chorus plods along
Listen for the counter song
Utterances in between
Dare to fathom what they mean

The acoustics of the main event
Play to shroud and to prevent
A message here from ringing true
Staff lines strain to let it through

Some combinations seem so strange
Flirting with a canine range
The sounds extracted, one by one
Add up to a story - done...?

Then appears the lyric sheet
Where acrid verse becomes so sweet
A changing word in just one line
From hand grenade to Valentine!

Only the seas shall change by Andrew Neil Carpenter

Swollen seas, the ship's disease,
Tease at every buoy and bell
And spill at will miasmal swill
Across the dark and fractal shore.
Teeth of rock outcrop and shock
Each passing bilious navy swell,
Which crash to land to scar the sand
That's torn across the ocean floor.

With endless wheeze, the saline breeze
Displeases all who wander on
The dunes, the beach, both leached and bleached
By jagged winds of sharp contour.
But just one man is swayed to stay,
To bear a yoke and not abscond;
He shall not flee these swollen seas,
They're all he has worth living for.

In broken fleece he watches on.
With furrowed brow he sits alone.
By wind unstirred, he rests inured
To every whim of Neptune's jaw,
And through his stand upon the strand
The sins of man shall be atoned
And rested as the anchored stone,
Bound forever on the shore.

Forever.
For only the seas shall change.

Sands by Eric Keizer. From his book *'Vignettes'*.

Hourglass time,
Sands of fate slowly move.
Implacable in silence.
You still remain a mystery.
Although I hear your voice,
everywhere.
You can't see the darker side,
The thoughts of shifting deserts,
Barren, vast,
Immovable
The Giza in my soul.
I run across the burning ground,
While you shift beneath my feet,
And leave me thirsting
For your touch,
While my eternity creeps forward,
grain by grain,
Burrowing in the crevices
Of my craggy face,
Burying me, shoulder high,
and exasperated, at the
Non - emotive,
And faceless.

Jacaranda: Blue on Blue by Laurie Grove

Every week she passes
Beneath me on her way
From the clinic in Kampala.
She rests awhile in my arms,
And marvels at the sky
Through the veil of my bloom;
Blue on blue.

The southern wind lullaby's
Through my branches; it sings:
"Stay little sister. You have
Many miles before home,
Before Lake Victoria laps
At your feet like a puppy
To welcome you back.

In your pack you carry
The medicine for mother.
Lay it down. I will stay guard.
I do this for others. Lay on my
Moss carpeted bole and sleep,
While I scatter my trumpets
To take home as a gift".

I have looked for her
For many days now.
I know the meaning
Of her absence. She will not come;
Her mother no longer
Needs the medicine; she is spared
The ten-hour round journey.

She will walk to the shore instead,
Yards from her shack,
And she will throw my blossom
Into the lake of her ancestors:
In remembrance of a mother,
And for a childhood gone;
Blue on blue;

I, Jacaranda offer shelter
To the weary; many arms
Wrap themselves round
My old gnarled skin,
And many tears nourish
The sap in my veins.

Many stories of fear and loss
Drop from trembling lips,
In the silence of my shade.
Small faces press tight against
My wrinkled body for the comfort
Only a grandmother can give.

I hear and learn much.
Sometimes, when storms come,
I rage and shake my branches,
As my sister-wind howls
With me through the night
For those who never return.
By morning I am broken.
My boughs stoop,
And I cry in the dew of dawn.

New travellers come,
As others journey no more,
And are lost to me.
I take the census
Of the sick and dying,
Numbered by my pretty
Blue flowers, strewn
Over the dust and rocks,
Shearing off the breeze,
Or washed up on lake shores;
Blue on blue.

33

Armistice by David John Terelinck

My paper is heavy with thousands
of fleeing refugees, smog from rising

emissions, an op-shop of broken
election promises.

Not yet seven, with presses still cooling
down from their weekend run,

my tabloid's musty with yesterday's news.
This Sunday rag behaves like Gypsy

Rose Lee, shedding flimsy articles
of garb for unwary suburban voyeurs.

Cheap newsprint migrates from paper
to finger to cup. Small cankers of blight
from the Gulf left behind
on my butter knife. My napkin bears

silent witness to a smudge of corruption
from the latest incumbent.

Bathrobes around the country are pilling
with statistics from the latest

terror attack, stained by the carnage
from a Las Vegas shooter.

Sounds of you bullying your way
into the day infiltrate

my broadsheet brooding.
I read of Kim Jong-un's

ballistic missile; you slam doors
and drawers, offer a brief invective
of obscenity, launch into another
toilet-seat-up-tirade.

the crash of plastic upon porcelain
and you clump your way down the stairs.

Lips pursed, leftovers
from last night's argument still clin
to the corners of your mouth.
Spilled milk and breadcrumbs,

war crimes of domesticity,
destroy the ceasefire of irritable

silence. Our granite-top DMZ
disappears beneath a salvo

of censure, a strafing attack
on my ability to care for anyone
other than myself.
How do I tell you of famine's

effect upon me? Or the image of a boy,
no more than twelve, holding

a machete and a severed head
in a war-torn street? Instead

I simply say sorry for my infractions,
and dance to your tune because you
can't hear the songs that I do
sung in the key of Aleppo.

Armistice won 2nd place, the Glen Phillips
Poetry Prize in 2018. The Peter Cowan
Writers Centre,

Two Tankas, by David Terelinck,

from his book *'Slow Growing Ivy'*.

Impossible
To brew fragrant tea
In tepid water –
Listening for your voice
In the temple bell at dawn

*   *   *   *   *

we find comfort
in slow turned pages
and spinning globes ...
year in, year out
the constancy of us

Going Home by Susannah Bailey

With brief enthusiasms, little more than verbal spasms
The guard shouts 'all aboard the (muffled) train'
'And the next stop is (inaudible again)'
A baby howls, my neighbour scowls
Exhaling cheese and onion
Cheese and onion
Cheese and onion

The fields and hamlets, lowering sky,
Graffitied bridges, hedges fly
With the flickering reflection of my face
We rattle onwards to my favourite place
And I am leaving London
Leaving London
Leaving London

Suddenly we're in reverse
Something strange and quite perverse
I may be wrong but it's not right
Under words that aren't polite
I hear thud thud not clackety clack
Clackety clack
Clackety clack

There's rain, or leaves, upon the track
We can't go on, we can't turn back
And a bus is quite insane,
On this quiet one-cart lane

37

One cart lane
One cart lane

Train and bus and train again
Change and change and change and then
All frustration and the miles
Are washed away in tears and smiles
Tears and smiles
Tears and smiles

Divine Amazon by Laurie Grove ©

A shard of ice in shadow
Through the thin night air.
She catches the thermals
To swoop in shallow dive
Across the swirling snow
That dusts the stars with vapour trail,
From the howling peaks
Above lonely Arequipa,
And the high Inca plains,
In that rare space before space
Where the earth arcs and shimmers.
Spectral, almost invisible,
But for her silver tipped wings
That outshine the constellations
In their slow tumble to dawn.

She soars snowdrift and rockslide,
Over Puno down to Lake Titicaca,
Clipping the waves,
Wind foam in her crest,
As Cassiopeia dances off
The dark mirrored surface;
Feathers brushing the sand
Along the shoreline, in search
Of carrion to carry home,
Among the rocks and bare tree line,
To the lightning struck bole

39

Of blasted oak, where her young
Chitter and squawk.

But home is not for much longer,
The chicks are almost grown.
In time, she will mate again,
A clawed frenzy on the wing,
In parabolic dive
Of instinctive feral release,
Before the final moment,
Seconds from the ground, then back
Up to the solitude she craves.
She cares little for the ways of men.
There is no sophistry in her body.
She has seen Pisaro come and go,
Atawulpa vaunt to her godhead.
Unchanged as the Andean skyline,
Perfectly evolved in eye and wing,
Exquisite in beak for tearing flesh.
First to greet the morning sun,
Reflected in her red copper eye.
A proud, fierce, lonely huntress,
Rarefied and out of this world.
Condor - the divine Amazon.

Sentimental Value by Ruby Pond

Who am I?
Am I merely an object; insignificant?
Have I not served thee well
In all occasions?
I admit, on wobbly legs
I struggled to find my place,
whilst you moved me from corner to corner
to find the perfect spot.

My presentation of the utmost importance
for that first meet and greet
all those many years ago.
The soft fine linen draped upon my spine
folded out in soft curves along my edges
with lace doilies dressing me up to meet
fine wine and silver

as they mingled in wait for the entrée.
And I - pressed up in excellence and pride
to prove my worth in sturdiness
and host to good conversation and sated palates.
It was the night of a virgin presentation...
In the morning, bare and naked,
still in shock from the removal of my laced dress
the evening before, I once again stood strong
for a different sort of gathering.

41

My outer presentation
almost immediately dulled and smudged
with sticky fingers, driblets of milk and tiny rings of
oats
scattered across me in random patterns.
Followed by a vigorous washing
where giggles and chatter lingered
in the lines of my wood
building my character though out the years.
My versatility was my strength,
And my availability – you were all privy to
At the mercy of your good grace
And housekeeping skills
Alas, to all who gathered around me,

In the comfort of my stableness
And chose to hold
one-sided telephone conversations
catnap on my surface
and prop against me
and I in turn supported you all
Providing your most basic needs
Catching crumbs and tears and reflections of smiles
My dings, my scratches, like scabs and scars
more precious with each passing year.
So, sentimentally speaking, I ask
who am I?
Am I merely a piece of furniture?
Or am I a part of this family?

Temper Tantrum - a Rondeau chain by Ruby Pond

I blew my lid when things got tough
A battle raged, the fight was rough
A blind attempt, two fisted try
A rip and tear straight through the eye
This shell it left, not quite enough
I blew my lid

Now compromised, me in a huff
My ruckus made just off the cuff
A better breath exhaled cause I
Did blow my lid

Oh, guess I'd need some potent stuff
To fix my skin – a powder puff
With magic potion, so applied
To look another in the eye
Yet, damage done, now left to sigh
-I blew my lid

If I'd just learned to hold it in
Reigned in my fury, my patience thin
If only I had kept control
I wouldn't need to be consoled
If I'd just learned

Yet, burst it did, my dam broke in
The battle lost, I couldn't win
If I'd have captured looks I stole
When wits were gone and I bared soul
Regret then surfaced, and sucked me in
If I'd just learned

Now, look at me, my arms all crossed
A speck in eye, these guts all tossed
The ruin of face and shame to bear
A situation beyond repair
Yet, own the right to bear the cross

This vessel now a total loss
I blew it good – just like a boss
Somehow it seems it isn't fair
(don't look at me)

My temper, it did double cross
Reputation – a mighty cost
Seems, burst it did with quite a flair
My fragile parts are everywhere
The efforts made sure to exhaust
A look at me

Pitter ... Patter ... Pitter ... Patter

A La'Tuin - By Miriam Ruff

There are whispers in the woods at night
Shadowy creatures out to play
Little do we understand what's said their soft patter
gives us fright

In such pitch blackness we lose our sight
Colors first drain and turn to gray
Unblinking are the large eyes quite red
On dank air like some great blight

There's no decision, we cannot fight
We hold our breath and start to pray
Into the silence we're quickly led
Our faces pale, our aspect white

What will we learn there, what great insight
That comes from darkness, not from day
And while on sacred grounds we do tread
Those voices give us no delight

There are whispers in the woods at night
Shadowy creatures out to play
Little do we understand what's said
Yet their soft patter gives us fright

Portents - A Rondel Prime by Miriam Ruff

How will history view us when we are all dead
When the last of our air turns to dust in the sky
Will they know what has happened without asking
why
Or will all be as clueless as our lot instead

Even now the sky turns a strange new shade of red
While we dither and dicker and make up our lies
How will history view us when we are all dead
When the last of our air turns to dust in the sky

Our great planet we're ripping into tiny shreds
And large portions of land are so bone-sucking dry
In the heat of the sun we will be apt to fry
And we're now just encased in a mountain of dread
How will history view us when we are all dead
The great future we planned will not wait up ahead

Decaffeinated Fairy Lights by Samantha Beardon

Bring us words - witty, wise or wistful
Written with all their potential
Make sense of life's distorted mirror
To unlock your deepest emotional stirrings
Write with all your potential

Share your words - wrapped in plastic, paper or silk
Extract understanding, pain and happiness
As you touch the deepest pit, your wildest joy
Help us distill each drop of emotion
Bitter, sweet or salty combinations
on the tongue then, project films –
romance to noir from amidst your potential

Trumpet music and songs with your words- fanfares
of feelings
From decaffeinated fairy lights to surging seas
Mix words with the music from your soul
Find metaphors from the wellspring of experience
Words from broken shoes to purring Ferraris
That elicit a thickened throat, a glimmering smile
The sigh that escapes lips after reading.

Paint as Picasso, Turner, Bacon -Sketch your words
Those written from the well spring of your potential.

In Darkness Rising – A Ravenelle by Miriam Ruff

Follow me into the sadness, where you'll find there's naught but madness,
Dreams forsaken in the pit, I'm shaken to the very core—
Once it seemed that life came calling, now it feels that I am falling,
Feelings that to me are galling, trapped with darkness wanting more.
Lost to me is my salvation, life in pain is what's in store—
Pain in waves and always more.

When was life yet filled with brightness, when were things all tinged with rightness,
In the distant past I flourished, happy times were still at hand—
Then came thoughts all filled with sorrow, never gone from day to morrow,
No bright light could I e'er borrow, no safe place could I still land.
Lost to me was hope and promise, thoughts constricted like a band—
Life and sorrow hand-in-hand.

"Who I am." by Yahya A. Gimba.

I am a poet

    I see through the asthenic bones of hungry men,

    Women and their Seed—I see beyond your attires

I am a poet

    walking on thorns, to carry my head

to the throne of power

    Towards a future hanging in the mouths of
sparrows

I am a poet

    finding peace in walking back my footprints

    And inspiration on the stomachs murmuring

    and singing from hunger

    I see beyond the light faces you wear at mid-days

I am a poet

    Ashamed of seeing the hands

strangling poetry to death,

    stabbing 'her' so deeply with swords

I am a poet

    I wasn't born a poet

I was made one

    And taught to see through poetic lenses.

Seafarers not quite a sonnet by David Bray

Shellback sailor, Liverpool fireman
Lookout, helmsman, stewards too
Bosun, chippy, gold-lace captain
ABs, greasers, all one crew
All away from home enduring
Long night watches, boredom lays
Heavy on endless ocean crossings
With hectic fever in haven days
Convenience flag, strange registry
Fair weather and foul, in peace and in war
Brings you your butter, bananas and tea
Merchant seamen, it's what we're here for
Serve Master and owner, at times uncomplaining
To all others invisible, us heroes at sea

****

Rhyme doesn't have to be a crime
It has a place just not all the time
Poesy must always flow
Let other devices having a go
Free verse has to have rhythm
Or it's prose no algorithm
Bad rhyme is often the issue
It just doesn't - kiss you!
Samantha Beardon

51

Let me tell you

Narrative Poem by: The_Living_Legend ©Iamteazhy
from *The Street child (Series 1)*

This is my story and that of thousands of others who have no voice:

Let me show you my bruises visible and invisible,

Let me show you my scars, how life buzzes and stings,

Let me show you how I gaze up to the stars, as I

Call to my ancestors, for solace, to extend their wings.

Nobody cares about the life of a child who lives on the street,

I am a child with no childhood, without love, vulnerable meat,

Let me show you a time living with my family and merry dreams,

that have drowned in life's chaotic alligator streams.

Let me show you the pain of a 12-year old losing a mother,

See me, no home left to survive, alone with no other,

*Let me show you how I dine, on rotten food,
disgusting tastes,*

*My food shared with dogs, leftovers from street
side wastes.*

*Let me show you my tears, my anguish how bad it
hurts,*

Remembering I have no hut, just a small piece of dirt,

to lay my head, no story, no kiss so much to miss,

Let me show you the nightmare of horror and despair

*At the mercy of the unscrupulous no skills just
prayer.*

Let me tell you how I repeat those rhymes,

I hear from kids who go to school, ordinary times,

Whenever I peep through the school window,

*I try to hear, to learn - as my tears flow like those of
a new widow.*

*Let me show you how flies feast on my wounds like
ghouls,*

See my shivering, as malaria rips off my soul,

See how I sweat in the midday sun as I am forced to

labour, chasing streetcars with goods on my head,
could you?

Let me show you how sickness pays me homage,

How my feeble minds lacks courage,

How I sleep on the chilly floors of abandoned huts in
the rain,

How I shiver with a palpitating heart as I live with
the strain,

A street kid with no defenders, no money torn apart.

Does it touch your heart? My street life's way?

How I look forward to having a better day,

Not because I want to be praised,

You need to know I am differently raised.

 Not nurtured with a silver spoon,

I am a wolf, life changed me to a poltroon,

As a street child my life is so miserable

But still, I crave to someday to have a life, shake the table.

To all street children out there, don't get lost in life wild winds, just because you come from the dirt doesn't mean you can't be clean, we all have a story to tell in the nearest future, fight hard to create a good and inspirational story so the world out there will talk about you as a hero, a legend.

*

n

Vital Spark - a Sonnet by Samantha Beardon

The composition sets a vital spark

The artist's hand unseen, forever hid

This study blazing, shaded red to dark

With waves of passion -artist's eye undid

She sits immortalised inside the frame

A picture frozen cold but feeling warm

The tones depict his love connect the flame

The artist holds an image to transform

The need to paint compulsion getting strong

His vision blurs his world begins to shrink

The painter deaf to breeze and natures song

His mood I guess as dark as blackest ink

The image weeps the brush occludes the tears

A slave imprisoned - spells he used for years!

What is poetry?

Poetry is a form of art that enhances the musicality of language and should be a vehicle to enlighten, move, excite its readers.

Stop for a moment and think what poetry means to you, how you see it. Jot down your ideas and see if they have changed by the end of the chapter; what do you think poetry is and is not? List any features that you might expect to find in a poem.

'Writing a poem is like *trying to find a black cat in a room where no lights are switched on.* And you know you've touched it, but where was it, where ... (and even though you touched it, it's probably moved!)' *Anon.*

Defining poetry precisely is rather the same. A poem is the best expression of what the poet wants to say.

What poetry is, is a question you will ultimately have to answer for yourselves. There are many definitions and many ways of looking at poetry. You have already seen in our initial reading that it comes in all shapes, sizes and genres.

The big issue with the arts in general is that there are many different genres and each genre has people polarised in their views about whether the piece of art makes the genre at all and if so whether it works as a piece of art. If it makes the genre - whether it's a love - hate relationship.

Let's look at music: I love much classical music although some music I find irritating, unfulfilling and uncomfortable to listen to. I love rock music; I grew up with it, it pulses through my blood. Folk music has great tunes and often memorable stories, rhymes, rhythms. I like jazz, some modern pop and hip hop. You get the picture; music is a bit like poetry, it is not really one thing. The different parts all have their fans and often the fans positions are polarised. Everybody will have different views.

The art of poetry resides in technical detail more than one might like to believe. The writer artfully uses technique with the express purpose of getting you to feel what he or she wants you to feel. The poet manipulates emotions and sound just as a composer may write a piece of music to evoke a particular mood. The composer orchestrates not only the instruments but also the listener. This is the case in poetry too.

There is no "accepted" definition of what a poem is. Many people will tell you there is, but they are wrong. Most poets or writers on poetry have formulated their own ideas and definitions, usually to exclude the areas of poetry they do not like, but that is all they are ideas. Poetry is not about rhymes, but it might be. Poetry is not about metre, but it might be. Poetry doesn't follow one format.

There are few rights and wrongs. Many opinions. There are principles of good poetry practice and we will be exploring them throughout the next few chapters.

What you have is poetry that falls into different categories

- Rhyming poetry – that where each end line rhymes but is not written in a special form.
- Free verse – poetry that doesn't have a regular rhyme or metre.
- Classical forms – poetry where rhyme schemes and metre are proscribed for example Sonnets, Odes, Ballads, Rondeaus.

Real poetry doesn't always say anything concrete or literal although it might; it just ticks off the possibilities, opens all doors. You can walk through anyone that suits you. Poetry uses a mixture of literal and figurative language and other poetic devices to tell its stories.

What we can do is look at different ways to define what poetry is, explore its sources and ways in which to write original poetry.

Poetry can transform, change perspectives, move us to a different place, astonish us. Poetry is art, it's music, it's light and darkness. Entering a good poem, a person feels, tastes, hears, thinks, and sees in altered ways.

Poetry is exciting, liberating, and versatile; you can be artistic, use sounds, patterns and pictures. Patterns of words and sounds build any number of different pieces. You can use concrete imagery, abstract imagery and write with wild abandon There are few real rules but what we do have are tools that can help us to write poetry which stands out from the crowd. These are the things we need to explore.

Is poetry mostly about the expression of feelings? No. One common misconception is that its function is simply this.

Does poetry tell the absolute truth; as true an account as possible akin to a journalistic account? Probably not. Poetry works differently. Our personal lives and history inform our work, but the poem transforms or exchanges the one sort of truth – biographical truth – for another: poetic truth. A poem is more than a simple expression of feelings, more than what 'really' happened.

The following chapters will help you become familiar with those tools and the principles on which you can build your poetic masterpieces.

You can go online and find hundreds of definitions of poetry.

Over the years, poets have been asked for definitions and here are some of them:

"A poem is human inside talking to human inside."

> *Donald Hall, editor. Claims for Poetry. p142.*
>
> *University of Michigan Press. (2002)*

This quote suggests that poetry is a bridge, a mode of communication that is intimate and speaks of being human.

"Poetry: three mismatched shoes at the entrance of a dark alley."

> *Charles Simic. Dime Store Alchemy. The Art of Joseph Cornell (New York Review Books Classic)*

This quote goes toward the notion of poetry as something concrete and yet slightly mysterious which draws you in:

"that unconscious store cupboard in the brain..."
Anon

Speaks for itself, the transmission of information stored and almost forgotten.

"But poems are like dreams: in them you put what you don't know you know."

> *Adrienne Rich. When We Dead Awaken.:*
> *ReVision. Essay (1972.)*

This quote is suggesting the wellspring from which poems come.

"I have said that poetry is the spontaneous overflow of powerful feelings: it takes its origin from emotion recollected in tranquillity: the emotion is contemplated till, by a species of reaction, the tranquillity gradually disappears, and an emotion, kindred to that which was before the subject of contemplation, is gradually produced."

> *William Wordsworth, Harriet Wordsworth,*
> *Poems, p388; (1815)*

Here the suggestion is that whilst poetry springs from spontaneous emotion it should be written after a period of reflection.

"Poetry is the purest of the language arts. It's the tightest cage,

and if you can get it to sing in that cage it's wonderful."

Rita Dove. Poetry Flash (1993)

Poetry self-evidently is born out of speech. It's a written and spoken art where language is concentrated and distilled.

For me personally the essence of poetry is the use of concentrated language to make specific emotional responses through meaning, sound and rhythm.

Whether we receive something as a poem or not, also has to do with the set of expectations that come with being told something is poetry. It's a sort of contract between creator and audience, through which we create a particular kind of space for communication.

It can be helpful to be aware of poetry's roots in oral, pre-text cultures and its links to music, song, memory and ritual. Tales and 'voicings' functioned as a repository for cultural knowledge before people had access to the relative permanence of text. Poetry often still has a strong link to culture, tradition, community and memory. What qualifies as poetry (or as good poetry) can be quite culturally specific. It also changes over time.

Keep in mind the ideas about poetry here and explore your own definitions. You may like to list them all together, with each response on a different line. If you do this, you might even have a poem!

Exercise

Go out and explore some of the different ideas about what poetry is. You might get a few surprises.

What makes a poem work?

For a poem to work well it must work on a variety of levels. Here I am not talking about what someone likes or doesn't like but if on some level the poem works at all. As a general idea a mainstream modern poem would score highly on each of these points:

Authentic – is it saying something that has a ring of truth to it?

Accessible – readable, understandable.

Evocative – images that evoke the moment.

Engaging – do I want to read on, involve myself in this poet's world construct?

Interesting – perhaps even surprising, but with enough about it to make reading it worthwhile even if it doesn't appeal to me.

Musical – Sounds that are in concordance with the theme and message.

One thing to bear in mind is that poetry is dynamic; it is not a static vehicle. The poet sets up a poem so that it engages the ever-curious brain of the reader. Poetry is an interaction between poem and reader causing some sort of reaction. A poem's job is to move the reader in some way, be it excitement, revulsion, joy, sadness, exasperation or any other emotion other than boredom. If you read a poem and it doesn't move, you it has failed. It may be that you are too far away from its conception, or it has been clumsily put together. If there is no appeal to emotions or senses the poem has failed; it is just noise.

Art needs, life, movement. It needs to be made of music, not noise.

Exercise:

Which of these pieces of writing do you think are poems?

"Sitting on my office chair I hear the creak of leather as I settle my desk is in order my computer a notebook and pen arranged across the polished surface I pull a slate coaster from the holder in the well and place it away from the folder and the keyboard the aroma of Colombian coffee is teasing my nostrils and spiralling with the steam into the air then, opening the computer I check the statistics of Stat oil and Shell and as the figures appear on the screen a grin spreads across my face I'm on track to meet my projections my client will be pleased."

"Today my dream seems set to rust think it's past it reduced to dust gossamer threads colour my day looking at a horizon layered in grey sure the dark is pulling me in hold my dreams in my hand sift through their hues there a bright strand hold that strand towards the light twinkling green then pink burning bright sure the dark is starting to spin."

"Inner peace the eternal quest the object of our heart's desire the trait we most want to acquire the eternal quest for happiness object of our hearts desires the driver our search for love inspires."

Answers P363

Time for a few challenges to try in the coming weeks

Find a newspaper article that is a little unusual. Now think what it would have been like to experience the event first-hand. Explore the event using your imagination and your senses. Brainstorm the idea and turn it into a poem.

The next challenge requires a dictionary. Take a poem you have written and replace every noun within the poem with a word you take from the dictionary. Aim to go five or six words in front or behind the noun. Place the word in the poem and see what you get.

Find an old photograph something random you have forgotten about or something that holds more memories and write a poem based on the memories as a starting point.

How to begin writing poetry

Writing poetry should be a pleasurable activity which grows as your skills increase. So, find ways of writing that work for you and integrate into your work and home environment in ways that don't cause you stress.

The first step in any poem is coming up with something to write about. Don't feel that you must choose profound or "poetic" material. Anything can be the subject for a poem. Often small and very ordinary items can make a wow poem. Check out poems such as *'Mother Washing Dishes'* by Susan Myers.

Budget Air by Samantha Beardon

I am in a plane a few miles in the air
A passenger jet with no room to spare
I sit in a rare thing, the front row
a space with- room for my knees
My bum fits the seat with a just a little squeeze
I was worried before, because I knew
the plane seats are tiny, more space in a zoo
I had fingers and toes crossed, the seat belt would fit
It did, thank my guardian angel, I would have
felt like a twit
Luckily the flight is only short
A long haul in this wouldn't be sport

My arm is wedged against the curve in the wall
Understand how sardines feel, not having a ball
A means to end but an uncomfortable lack
Of reasonable comfort, give the designer the sack
I am sat in a plane a few miles in the air
We are descending oh YES nearly there!

Read poetry as much as you possibly can; look at styles and layouts which appeal to you. Whilst some people claim their 'muse' is a thing of their thoughts and to read the work of others would contaminate their work, if you go back to how you learnt to write, it was by imitation. Reading and listening to poems enable you to pick out the ways the poet instilled rhythm, emotion, and chose words. Even if to start with you totally copied the style you would use your own words and ideas, which would make it yours. However, you are more likely to experiment with ideas that appeal to you within your own work and it is this experimentation that will help you find your poetic voice.

A huge resource for writing poetry is yourself, much poetry has at least a smattering of the autobiographical.

We can use our own lives in poetry, in the way that artists might paint pictures of themselves. With imagination not necessarily actually writing about oneself in an obvious way, in the same way that an artist isn't necessarily painting a replica of themselves when they paint. You can change your history, change your past, change your memories and alter it, but it can be a springboard to ideas. Memories and observations are the raw materials for poets. Keep that notebook ready to jot down those thoughts when triggered.

There are a few different ways to go about writing a poem and it depends on your personality - the way you like to work which you will choose, although I recommend trying them all before settling on a method.

- Think of a topic and jump right in, writing the poem in a style you like.
- Think of a topic and brainstorm key ideas and words about the subject. Arrange the key ideas and words into a poem.
- Do 'stream of consciousness' writing; think of your subject and just write nonstop for five minutes. Don't think about what you are writing - just write. When your time is up, edit your writing and pull out the key themes and any key words. This will form the basis of your poem.
- Research your subject and find interesting facts or ideas to integrate into your poetry.

Use a notebook to jot down any ideas for poems you have, keep that book in your bag or pocket. Jot down that intriguing snippet of conversation, the annoyance, the sudden sparked idea.

Look at the world with new eyes. Be alert for imagery in ways you might never have been before. Think of comparisons between unlikely things. How do things look, sound, smell, feel or taste? Jot ideas in your notebook for later use.

Finding time to write is always contentious, we all have busy lives and competing priorities. If you want to write you will find a way. The ideal is to block an hour or two of dedicated writing time and build that into your schedule. There are also those unexpected small bites of time that you may 'waste' now. Luckily, poetry is a process well suited to being constructed in small chunks so you can plan a poem, write a line or two or edit on the bus, on a train, sitting in a waiting room, waiting for cooking to be completed, in the bath - I am sure you can find small bytes of poetry time in all hours of the day. Another area of poetic creativity!

Ideas for Poems.

Ideas are everywhere if you stop and think. Any aspect of everyday life can be the subject of a good poem, something a reader can empathise with. Walks, nature, beauty; all provide fertile ground.

Human behaviour is another great area watch the people in the queue, on the train, in the restaurant.

Memories trigger ideas for poems they may be the springboard to a different scenario, but they can be the spark.

The news or an issue that made you happy, mad or sad.

Exercise:
Here is a line from a poem:

Those times that I have for idle dreams.

Think about that line then start to write. Don't think and consider the way, just write lines; you are not worrying about making sense, just keep the first line in mind and write. If you catch yourself trying to work out where you are going stop and repeat the first line until you start again.
This is not a time to choose or sculpt, this is a time for unfettered writing.

73

Once you have come to stop, delete the base lines. You have now the basis the raw material to compose a poem. You can do this from any line in poetry or prose or from an object.

The idea is to have a fixed point from which to invent and improvise just as musicians do with a tune. What you have is the idea from the first line infused throughout the writing.

Keep this rough draft and turn it into a poem then refine it as you read the chapters of the book.

Why do poets write poetry?

• Poetry takes us out of ourselves and into different worlds. It can expand our horizons. We read and write poetry to discover something new; something untapped.

• Poetry can be cathartic and can help us deal with intense human emotion that can be hard to express by other means.

• Poetry is a powerful tool for self-expression.

• Poetry can enable poets and readers to share others experiences and see the world through different vision.

74

- We write poetry because we feel the need to write.

- Poetry is part of life's rhythms our lives are steeped in the minutiae of sound, imagery and poetry.

- Some poets use poetry to populate a cause, highlight social injustice, and call attention political events.

- To interact with others who pursue the same art.

Why do you write poetry?

Get the writing journey started

Exercises

With autobiography as a basis for much poetry now is the time to dive under the surface of your psyche and think about your life and experiences. Take your notebook and write a short personal statement around 400 words; if you want to write more that is fine, and chart some of the events in your life. Relationships, jobs, school, emotional highs and lows. This is a resource for you to mine for poetry. This can be the starting point of a poem that is not autobiographical in nature but uses an event, idea or emotion that springboards directly from your life. Here you will have a thousand ideas.

Tomorrow

I want you to write a short piece of prose describing a view through a window. Any window any view. Not one that is from your imagination but one in the present or an actual memory of a view from a window.

The day after

Look back to the poems you have been reading and choose a style that appeals to you. Jot down the details, line length, any rhyme, any word repetition.

The day after

Take the prose you wrote about the view from the window. Write a poem using the chosen style as a template.

Every tomorrow

Fit in some writing practice. Start with prose, move to poetry.

Lines, Stanzas and Structure

The combination of sounds and visual elements provides a poem's structure; the sum of all sound and visual form in a poem.

The word stanza in Italian means 'room' and groups of lines are often gathered with white space between them thus forming the rooms of the poem. Hence their name stanzas.

The craft of poetry has traditionally concerned itself with the sounds of the words and the meaning, but poems are also written, and the patterns developed in that visual field can't be overlooked if we are to concern ourselves with the full potential of the poem's structure.

The sound patterns of a poem are concerned largely with the rhythm and tone of the word, visual pattern and variation are geared more toward the poem's placement on the page although it will affect the way it is read too.

When a poem works as it should everything fits together, and all the elements work together.

Like a painter at a canvas, the poet when concerned with the visual patterning of the poem looks at how the poem sits on the white canvas of the blank page and how that visual structure creates patterns that can be used to create a richer poem.

Let's look at how David John Terelinck laid out the first stanzas of the poem *'Armistice'*.

My paper is heavy with thousands
of fleeing refugees, smog from rising

emissions, an op-shop of broken
election promises.

He used mostly couplets (2-line verses) with some short last lines, words clustered then spreading like those refugees across the page.

Short verses of two lines (small rooms) in this poem and lines symmetrical then broken. That short line pulling you into the next stanza.

Go back and look at the poem and its organisation and think about the layout in relation to content and meaning. Can you see any correlation?

Then think about these first lines; do they intrigue you, make you want to read more?

Lines

As you have been studying and reading poetry you will already be familiar with the line; that finite subdivision of the poem.

The discrete unit of words which may or may not be finished with punctuation. Whilst it's like a sentence it is not the same.

A poetic line rarely covers the full width of a page, it stops where the poet decides it will. A line doesn't necessarily follow the clause or grammatical structure of the sentence.

There is an ability to manipulate a line to enhance the sound, meaning or emotion of a poem.

The line breaks - the reader must turn back on themselves to start a new line even while the idea may be continuing. In Latin this is called versus, which translates as 'turn' and is where the word verse comes from.

It is important that line breaks are chosen with care. Get them wrong and they will skew understanding of a poem and even make reading difficult and annoying.

Remember that the end of a line is one of the strongest positions for words so think about word placement in your lines.

There is the suggestion that a line should be the length of a breath, so a long line leaves you breathless and short lines leave you hyperventilating. A thought to ponder.

We always pause at a line break, to breathe, think, adjust our momentum.

Line lengths can be used by the poet for a variety of functions.

Lines can be of the same length in a poem giving regularity, of varying lengths which can speed or slow reading down.

There can be a relationship between different line lengths.

If you start with a short line and then write a longer line, you match your shorter line and then extend it. This gives stability and can hold the poem the reading speed the emotion.

If you go from longer to shorter line lengths this pushes the story forward, there is less stability it can unsettle, heighten emotion.

Lines of equal length will maintain total stability and speed of reading.

The stability or lability of the emotions or ideas being expressed in your poem or stanza should influence your choices of line set-up.

Therefore, in Free Verse or free rhyming poetry your line lengths can be used to enhance your message if you are demonstrating love, happiness, pleasure. You are wanting a stable environment; you want your reader immersed in the action. If you are illustrating or building up to a breakup, a calamity, grief; a twist you can use is a sudden out-of-step line length or a less even pattern to add a jarring feel.

Here there is disruption, and this is echoed in the structure:

The normal pattern of her day
             disrupted
something is lurking in the air,
it feels drier and tastes acrid-
not foul but infused
with sulphur like the outer vestiges of hell.
She takes a deep breath trying to sift
  through the aromas, the deep earthy tones,

the mustiness of rotten vegetation,
overlaid with something indefinable,
immutable and worrying.

Line length can be measured in various ways by syllable count, by visual acuity, by word count.

Some examples of poems with stable and unstable line lengths:

This poem *The Island* has a variable syllable count, but the lines are visually the same length.

Island by Samantha Beardon

I am an island - I am unique

Full of brilliance and flaws

I am an island - my core beliefs

Like the magma of the earth

Bubble, seethe and coalesce

Those beliefs hidden deep

Here is part of a poem *Destruction*. It has 10 syllables (beats) per line and is a classic form called the *Terza Rima*. With lines grouped in threes, so stanzas of uneven length but regular line lengths.

Destruction – by Samantha Beardon

You are creator, destroyer, transformer
Which will you be, as you play your guitar?
I wanted love to be your reformer.

You spark and sizzle your essence a flare
You consume, it's your way of persistence
Your music, just one way, to lay souls bare.

This is part of the poem. It is another form with a set syllable (beat) count per line. Seven syllables with an extra three syllables on the first line of each stanza.

Castle magic – by Samantha Beardon. Englyn Penfry form.

I conjure it with magic- castle fair
Just don't stare, fall or panic
My creation huge gigantic

Floating in the air so near - carrion
Clarion call for all fear
Darkness not my plan be clear

I have miscalculated - magic dark
Foulness spark, my spell fated
Goodness, has dissipated

The next poem has lines that vary slightly in length
with the last three lines short and the last lines
arranged off centre.

I feel - by Samantha Beardon

I imagine you with every song that I hear
I feel your touch when my skin is kissed by the sun
I feel your breath as the breeze blows through the
window
I hear your voice in the distant roar of the train
I imagine you flying free when the owl hoots in the
night
I picture you; I feel you
                    You are there
                            I feel you.

How can we use line breaks to our best advantage?

Short lines sometimes speed things up; they certainly
add a staccato effect, but a long line can have the
effect of a headlong rush.

In Auden's poem *The Night Mail*, pace and train
sounds are added by the line length and the rhythm.
Find it on the Internet and listen to it.

Pace can be developed by using short vowel sounds, avoiding adjectives, as well as using onomatopoeia and images of speed.

Slower pace uses a less jerky iambic rhythm and a few long vowels, such as you would find in words like (brood, breeze, miles). Mainly it comes down to the rhythm of the lines and the shortness of the phrases, so for example if a line is written in short phrases it will appear to move faster than a line which has longer phrases, so you might have these lines.

on the old picture   thin spidery lines

marks branches   twigs and leaves

detail remains   hidden

To speed this up into something to be read faster you might edit it like this:

on a picture   spidery line

branches   twigs   leaves

details   hidden

Condensing and tightening the phrases into shorter bites will increase the speed of delivery, use of single words or short lines will also add to this effect. Longer phrases or multi syllable words will cause the poem to appear slower, removing and tightening and simplified language will increase its pace.

Remember:

Line breaks are like rests in music, a pause for breath.

Line breaks can add sound, music and tone.

They can also help create the emotions of joy, horror or sadness by moving us on, giving us resolution and stability, or leaving us with unresolved ideas.

Broken syntax …. makes the reader focus because it breaks patterns and disturbs our craving for order.

Enjambment - forces the reader to focus on the last word of the line.

Line breaks evoke a sensation (freedom, discomfort, excitement, etc.), perhaps by breaking the line in an unnatural place causing instability.

Impel the narrative forward, create room in which to expand a train of thought or idea.

Subvert or challenge existing conventions, if this suits the theme of the poem.

Lines can be end stopped, an idea might finish, or a pause is needed, those pauses are like punctuation. The poet decides to use formal punctuation or not. Whichever the choice is it should be consistent.

End stopped lines with punctuation

My love is not of the springtime,

Blossoms, nesting birds and new-born lambs,
Rising sap and sprouting leaf.

and without punctuation:

My love is not of the springtime

Blossoms, nesting birds and new-born lambs

Rising sap and sprouting leaf

Enjambment

Lines can have what is called an *enjambment*; the idea carries on to the next line.

- Enjambment is the insertion of a strategic line break.
- Enjambment must have purpose and is not to be used arbitrarily. It should be used to pull the reader through a short line to the next, where the thought can end on a weighty word capable of making the reader pause to absorb what has just been said.

- It should not cause the line to end on an article it should finish with a word with some weight that can carry the reader through to the natural stop.
- When used skilfully, enjambment will not only carry the reader's attention through the poem but will create tension in the piece that complements the connotations, imagery, or metaphors intended by the author.
- Enjambments can happen over two lines, several lines or even from one stanza to the next if the poet is skilful enough.

Enjambment examples.

In *Cultural Differences* we have a long line, thoughts broken into three lines the first two lines showing enjambment

Cultural Differences by Samantha Beardon

The values, practices, traditions, beliefs
shared within my community, shaped
my formative years within a structure.

In *Only the Seas will Change* you have a single description broken in two lines. You have organisation of sounds as well in the first line and a faster more jagged feel to the second line plus the instability brought about by that second short line.

Only the Seas will change by Andrew Carpenter

The dunes, the beach, both leached and bleached
By jagged winds of sharp contour.

In *Blue on Blue,* Laurie Grove has basically used two sentences broken down into seven short lines. The first two lines have enjambment; the sense carries on from one line to the next. The fourth line has been finished with a comma making a definite pause then we have an enjambment and a definite pause, so the poet is orchestrating the speed of reading and the organisation of phrases and continuity. The lines are basically even in length apart from the last line which is shorter, but finishes a picture and because of the repetition of *blue on blue* it gives us repetition which gives closure.

Jacaranda: Blue on Blue by Laurie Grove

Every week she passes
Beneath me on her way
From the clinic in Kampala.
She rests awhile in my arms,

And marvels at the sky
Through the veil of my bloom;
Blue on blue.

In Messages on page 91 the enjambment crosses stanzas and stanza breaks which is unusual but can be effective. It is unsettling and causes one to be pushed out of the poem and works well for uncomfortable subjects where you move ideas on swiftly. Is this the right stanza set up for this poem? I leave you to decide!

Messages by Samantha Beardon.

The messages
 and the pictures
seem to beguile
 and bewitch
us.
Add another layer
 to infinity
Bring us closer
 you and me.
The messages

 and the pictures
Fill in blanks
 remove the strictures.
They leave me
 breathless
Happiness endless
The you I see
Beguiles

 Me.
The messages
and the pictures
Sent to
 beguile
 Bewitch us.

Note the start of the lines, I have not started my
enjambed lines with a capital letter as I prefer to
show the fact that the line is a direct continuation of
the idea. Both Andrew and Laurie have chosen the
tradition of starting each sentence with a Capital
letter regardless of the fact some lines are
enjambments.

Neither is right or wrong; it comes down to personal
preferences. You choose the way that works for you,
just remember to keep to the same system throughout
a poem.

Exercise:

Read this piece and turn it into a poem, set your line
breaks and any enjambments to make it work. Try
out line lengths until you are happy. Try for some
consistency.

*Silence does it exist? can we define it? what does it
mean to each?*

*We can be silent make things silent if we exist is there
ever a true absence of sound. Quiet, muteness, peace,
tranquillity. Lack of sounds, all shades of silence,
unexpected quietness, if we exist is there ever a true
absence of sound? Silence but I hear thrum thrum
that insistent beat of my heart. Soft syllabic breathing
as I live never total silence.*

Exercise:

Read a poem and look at how the poet has used their lines, what effects have they achieved?

How are the lines ended?

Is enjambment used, and if so, what is its effect?

Opening Lines

To make a reader want to read a poem, the first line, or the first few lines need to be a great opening, or a hook to draw the reader in.

How have some of the writers in our reading poems tried to draw you into their poetry?

You're seeking forgiveness
I cannot begin
To peel back the layers
Of you under my skin.
*

Autumn dusk can be so seductive
crisply sneaking in
unawares of the clock's pointy hands
erasing the day's heat.

Here are some other opening lines. Would they draw you in?

We were happy going out
Enjoying life as lovers do.
*

the bird whispers
as the cloud rejoice
a fountain being renewed.
*

When culture is well mined and understood
In view, Differently or indifferently, we'll proud.
*

Like a battered bride   frightened and unable to
speak   at dusk restless and thrown   weep drown
and drag down.
*

Can you match me measure for measure?
will you be sensitive to my pleasure?
can you pull me, out of a web of distrust?

Lines need to interest, intrigue, hook the reader in.
Having looked at the examples above, what do you
think makes the ideal opening to hook a reader with
your poem? Vivid description? Action? A
rhetorical question? A metaphor? Or something
different? Write this down and I will ask you the
question towards the end of the book. Will your
answer be the same?

Stanzas

When we begin thinking about lines, they are often orchestrated into a larger unit, which we call a stanza. A stanza seems a lot like a paragraph, but it's not the same.

A stanza is a collective unit of lines and they come in all kinds of different lengths. Some poems use regular lengths of stanzas, some irregular.

Stanza Names

- A stanza of two lines is called a couplet
- A stanza of three lines is called a tercet
- A four-line stanza is a quatrain
- A stanza of five lines is called a quintet or sometimes a cinquain
- A stanza of six lines is called a sextet
- A stanza of eight lines is called an octet

Within a poem stanza length can vary; for instance some poems have a stanza of two lines followed by a stanza of four lines.

In Free Verse there can be an infinite variety of ways to add structure but in classical forms stanza length is usually set by the rules of the form.

Stanza Breaks

A line break is the part where a line ends in a poem. A stanza break is the white space that comes between two blocks of poetic text.

What does it do?

It can give the reader a breathing and thinking space. It can visually balance the poem. It can allow the poem to be organised to enhance sound or meaning.

Again, lines seem to correspond to sentences, and stanzas seem to correspond to paragraphs, but they are not precisely the same thing. How is a stanza different from a paragraph? Stanzas are often divided more to create a sense of structure around sound than a sense of structure around meaning.

In a paragraph, you tend to organize it all into one big block, but you can divide your meaning among several different stanzas, because what you're regulating primarily is sound.

Poets can experiment with different stanza lengths to create different effects breaking up the same poem into different stanza lengths to find the best organisational scheme for the words and message of the poem.

Stanzas made up of an uneven number of lines feel more unbalanced, unstable, uneven compared to stanzas of even length which feel more balanced, stable and resolved. This should influence your choice of stanza length. They should vary with the emotion and message of your poem. You shouldn't always churn out poems with the same structure; consideration of structure enhances message.

These are some of the most immediate characteristics of a poem. Many poems use lines and stanzas as a way of scoring themselves; the poem's sound and sense, how they organize and orchestrate different dynamics. We feel something when poems speed up and slow down, we want to move on, we want resolution. The brain is looking for patterns looking for order trying to recreate it.

But of course, there are exceptions. if you've ever written a prose poem, you'll see a poem that doesn't use line breaks. Instead, it uses the width of the page just like a prose piece from a novel. But even so, we still must think in terms of lines and stanzas. These are the most common ways that poems are distinguished from their prose cousins.

Exercise: Here are three versions of the same stanza. Do they read differently? Which works best? How would you arrange the poem?

1.

Look into the mirror what do I see,
The outer shell, that masquerades as me,
Get a little closer, stare into my eyes,
See an inner glow, flickering, burning
a surprise, this my inner light, the unvarnished me,
Stripped of pretences, burning ever bright,
Not the face I show the world, just visible at night.

2.

Look into the mirror
what do I see,
The outer shell that
masquerades as me,
Get a little closer, stare
into my eyes,
see an inner glow
flickering, burning a surprise,
This my inner light
the unvarnished me,
Stripped of pretences,
Burning ever bright,
Not the face I show the world
just visible at night.

3.

Look into the mirror what do I see?
The outer shell
that masquerades

98

as me,
Get a little closer,
stare
 into my eyes,
see an inner glow
 flickering-burning,
A surprise,
 this my inner light,
The unvarnished me
stripped of pretences,
burning ever bright
Not the face
 I show the world, just visible at night.

The difference in these three examples is mainly line break to change how the words are read, to change the line stability. Do you think that breaking into more stanzas would work?

To sum up: the structure of a poem has a purpose. It shouldn't be arbitrary. Whilst meaning is the prime demonstrator of emotion, motion also causes emotion. The way we set line length; stanza length directly effects our feelings when reading poetry. The poetry experience is enhanced by our journey and how we make that is influenced by the poetic structure. It speeds us up, slows us down, sets a seed of disquiet when the message is tranquil and has us anticipating a potential twist.

The structure of the poem can act like the music in a film; for instance, as the horse and rider gallops across the plain the music develops a flatter note from some sections. It doesn't distract us but it does stimulate a little warning in our brain we anticipate things might not be right. Then the shots ring out. Uneven line lengths or stanzas can have the effect of being unsettling too. Use them.

Exercise:
Take a poem and rearrange the stanza breaks to give a different structure, try reading the original and your altered version aloud. Think about whether your changes have affected the sound, flow and sense of the piece.

The poetry building

We know that poems are made of words
join them together to form
the foundations
Lines are the strength the string, elastic, flexible
which need -breaks to enable us to make
the variety of shapes we need to create rooms

Our building resonates –
the chimes reverberate and flow
through sculptured channels

100

into the internal space creating
synergy - heating and electrifying.

Our building sleek and modern
With rooms custom built or formed
for a hotch-potch of functions
They can be grouped together
 or divided in creative ways
        into equal
or unequal sections these stanzas ...
may contain one idea
coalesce our sound system or
channel us along escalators
towards the pinnacle
the focus be it roof, dome,
tower, minaret or infinity.

Visual Art

Words, lines and stanzas are the foundations of our
poetry; they can also help as visual art too. Poetry can
be a piece of Visual Art. Whilst poetry has an aural
tradition, we also read it and look at it. Therefore,
you should consider the look of your poem as well as
the way it sounds. Poetry should be visual art as well
as giving musicality and flow. Therefore, the poet
needs to also consider the visual aspect of the poem.

For instance, if the words of the poem are centred it can suggest a spine of ink down the centre of the page, with the white space encroaching on it.

The poet can manipulate the spaces between words, between letters, can increase white space which can affect the looks and potentially the meaning of the poem.

Look into the mirror
    What
        do I see,
The outer shell
      that
  masquerades
              as me,
Get a little closer,
        stare
      into my eyes,
        see an inner glow
flickering,   *burning*
    a surprise,
This my inner light
      the unvarnished me,
Stripped of pretences,
   Burning
     ever bright,
Not the face
       I show the world
          just visible at night.

102

Here is *Look into the Mirror,* making use not just of different length lines but of different spacing and maximising white space. Alignment of a poem can also change the perspective

Here it is with centre alignment

Look into the mirror
What
do I see,
The outer shell
that
masquerades
as me,
Get a little closer,
stare
into my eyes,
see an inner glow
flickering,   burning
a surprise,
This my inner light
the unvarnished me,
Stripped of pretenses
Burning ever bright,
Not the face
I show the world
just visible at night.

And if the poem is aligned to the right this might
instil a sense of instability, with the reader casting
their eyes about looking for the start of each line
which is floating in space rather than aligned left,
where we usually expect to find it when
reading. There is research to suggest right alignment
is something better not done because it is
disconcerting to the eye. I leave you to think about
that and if there would ever be a case for using it.

> *Look into the mirror*
> *What*
> *do I see,*
> *The outer shell*
> *that*
> *masquerades*
> *as me,*
> *Get a little closer,*
> *stare*
> *into my eyes,*
> *see an inner glow*
> *flickering,* *burning*
> *a surprise,*
> *This my inner light*
> *the unvarnished me,*
> *Stripped of pretences,*
> *Burning*
> *ever bright,*
> *Not the face*
> *I show the world*
> *just visible at night.*

104

Poetry placement on the page is another dimension to consider when writing poetry and making it work with free verse. The length of line, line placement and use of white space, the position of the poem on the page are all important. In addition to your imagery, words, metaphors and message in making a poem sing.

When, as poets, we start to think of poetry in terms of meaning, sound and visual art we must think hard about the poem's structure. Getting the structure wrong, jarring white space, annoying placing of a poem on the paper, seemingly unconnected stanzas are likely to deter readers so with everything in life a balance is needed.

Concrete (shaped) Poetry

There is also a specific genre called *Concrete* or *Visual* Poetry. Concrete poetry is an arrangement of linguistic elements in which the typographical effect is more important in conveying meaning than verbal significance. It is sometimes referred to as visual poetry, a term that has now developed a distinct meaning of its own:

Poetry in which the meaning or effect is conveyed partly or wholly by visual means, using patterns of words or letters and other typographical devices.

This type of poetry has been used for thousands of years, since the ancient Greeks began to enhance the meanings of their poetry by arranging their characters in visually pleasing ways back in the 3rd and 2nd Centuries BC.

Concrete poems are objects composed of words, letters, colours, and typefaces, in which graphic space plays a central role in both design and meaning. Concrete poets experimented boldly with language, incorporating visual, verbal, kinetic, and sonic elements.

While it is important to note that there is no single definition of concrete poetry, the concrete poems that emerged from the international movement that began in the 1950s in Europe and South America do share important defining characteristics.

Concrete poets were masters of subtlety and reduced language, creating poems from very few words (or sometimes, a single word) which they then manipulated, permutated, and transformed. In Ian Hamilton Finlay's *Cork/Net*, four concentric circles are composed of only five words: cork, net, ring, price, fish, forming the shape of a net cork (a type of float used in fishing). The poems challenge our linear methods of reading. In Cork/Net, where does one begin? Where does one end?

Poems can also be written in the shape of an object.
To do this one can draw the shape on a piece of paper
and fill in the words, draw on a computer screen and
fill with words:

I look in
The   mirror   and
I

See my face

A
Triangle
Has three angles
And three sides most times
Different types have different shapes

As you can see concrete (shaped) poetry is not my
thing, mainly because my computer skills don't mesh
with my ideas, those with the skills create all sorts of
wonderful designs. I leave you to take concrete
poetry to new heights.

You will find many examples of poems in concrete
forms; flowers, wine glasses, question marks.

Look at examples on the internet and if your
computer skills are up to it give this genre a try.

this were a poem   it would be about wine
and it is shaped like a glass of wine.
Perhaps it is about
a   glass
of sec
or
or
or
just about the joy of wine

Sounds in Poetry

Poetry comes from an oral tradition; the earliest poems were recited or sung and were a way of remembering and passing on historical events and tales. In order to make them easy to remember mnemonic devices such as patterning in sound and rhythm and rhyme were used. In the early twentieth century vers libre or free verse came into being. Free verse changed poetry from strict metre and rhyme giving the chance for greater musical flexibility. This has obviously changed poetry; poets use a series of different devices to get musicality. Words and the musicality of their sounds are integral to all forms of poetry.

As poets we use words to paint pictures, we use concentrated language carefully chosen to produce imagery and ideas.

Words and their use are our stock in trade. We need to understand their use so well that we use them with skill.

Whilst poetry is more a written medium these days it still needs to be designed for the ear and the eye. If you want to write songs, getting the sounds right is imperative but is a combination of words and music. With poetry you have only the musicality of the words with which to capture your audience to bring your message to life.

We all have an inner ear too - the part of our brain translating what we are reading combines sight and sound.

Words are the way all of humankind communicates.

Words are comprised of letters; those letters all have sounds and combined they make the sound of our words.

We often talk automatically, we listen automatically, we forget how words are made, how we emphasise words or parts of words when we are trying to get a message across. How each part sounds as our ears hear and our brains translate.

Words are inherently musical if we listen to somebody speaking in a foreign language, we hear that musicality very clearly but because in our own language we are more concerned with meaning and nuance the musicality is still in evidence if we tune to it. We can also hear syllables more clearly.

When we speak our words rise and fall, our ears hear those sounds and translate them to meaning. When we speak our mouth, tongue and voice box move and change shape to produce the sounds. You can feel the shape and taste of words on your tongue.

110

Exercise:

Listen to somebody speaking in the language in which you write poetry, tune in to the sound, feel the rise, fall, emphasis of the words, note the musicality that you take for granted. Try to fade out the sense of the words and listen to the cadence. Then tune back into the meaning. Then listen for any patterns in the speech, word or phrase repetitions.

Because sound is made by the movement of air in response to muscular activity, speech and poetry are not just intellectual acts, but physical ones. When you read a poem aloud you are not just hearing the words and interpreting the stories, your whole body is involved in producing the sounds required to deliver the poem.

Let's go back to the basics of speech. The way we write things is not always how we say them.

In Poetry we make use of the sounds of the letters, particularly the vowels, to give us meaning, musicality, rhythm and flow. To rhyme we need to understand how vowels sound, because perfect rhyme is about the Identical Sound of the stressed syllable and any subsequent consonants in two words. In

111

Assonance we place words with the same syllable sound in proximity in a line.

In English the symbols for letters are the alphabet 26 in all. There are 5 vowels in English a, e, i, o, u. but over 20 vowel sounds. Vowels make sounds singly or in pairs called diphthongs or sometimes trios called tripthongs.

Then there are 21 consonants each with their own sounds.

In English there is not a total match of letters and sound.

Sounds often change due to the part of speech, the connotation or myriad other factors which we learn as we learn to read and speak.

For example, the words *bough, through* and *trough* all end in *ough* but each is pronounced differently! Factors like this can make rhyming difficult.

So, for us poets, an awareness of sounds and their tension becomes a key element in our toolboxes.

As you know vowels and consonants are the building blocks of words and sentences. In order to study the sounds of English, linguists devised an alphabet which contains symbols to capture all possible sounds in English, called the International Phonetic Alphabet. This is used in dictionaries and used to

112

teach reading and is a good way of understanding the sounds. It is worth reminding yourself of how phonetics is used in dictionaries, as it can help you become reacquainted with the sounds you are orchestrating.

Exercise:

Look up some words in a dictionary. Work through the phonetic spellings and compare the written transcript.

Check out an online syllable checker look up some multisyllabic words and see the syllable breakdown.

Music in Poetry.

If we mean 'music' as in 'music' rather than some indefinable thing from a poetic muse, then it means the poem portrays some deliberate organisation of sound by the poet. If there is some music within the poem that cannot be attributed to specific phenomena or devices, then it is likely to be due to the musicality that normally resides inside language. Having done the listening exercise you will understand that the musicality of your language is considerable. In normal speech we will make choices and go for harmonious options automatically. We regularly use metaphors, similes and clichés, all of which tend to give musicality.

Language is used and manipulated to bring out musicality and memorability. This often comes from how sound is put into patterns.

Think of the ad slogan that sticks in your mind, your favourite clichés and work out what adds music. Why does any of this matter to people writing poetry?

In poetry we should be building on the normal musicality of language musicality adding layers, of heightened music and heightened meaning and we do this through careful consideration of word choice. Music in poetry is one of the important threads in the effectiveness of poetry.

The sounds of words and parts of words, their rise and fall are an integral part of the poet's toolbox. A tool that many poets don't use to their full advantage.

Think of a continuum with normal speech at one end and poetry at the other, and prose between; this is how musicality should escalate.

Whether you write Free Verse or Classical forms, poetry is different to prose and needs fluidity, concentrated language and the use of sound to make it extraordinary.

For instance, perfect rhyme is based on the sound of the stressed syllable and any following consonants.

Poetry, that we see as musical has two main characteristics demonstrating repetition and variation – similarity and difference, conditions our brains search for all the time.

We have the variation of stressed and unstressed syllables and the patterning of consonant sounds. Vowels give the lift, the bulk to words. Consonants carve them into distinct entities of meaning.

Looking at the written word, the strength of the vowel is reduced, and consonants have more weight. This can reduce the power of musicality. Therefore, word choice is of paramount importance to maintain the music. Those alterations in pitch we call rhythm raise alterations to comprehension and mood.

Noise can be characterised as sound without structure or meaning. Antonyms for music are cacophony, discord, disagreement apply those same terms to lack of musicality in poetry.

Using Euphony to enhance your writing skills.

The literary device *euphony* is derived from the Greek *euphonos* and is about the psychological effects of sound and musicality.

Names and words are made up of sounds and each sound has natural meaning. In lots of cases the very shape of the letters is in accord with the sounds they produce. Whilst linguists might raise their eyebrows as a poet it is something worth considering. We should always be aware of the esoteric qualities the feelings produced by the sound and sometimes the look of a letter.

Sounds in poetry can help imagery and emotional build up.

Euphony gives pleasing and soothing effects to the ear due to repeated vowels and smooth consonants. It can be used with other poetic devices like alliteration, assonance and rhyme to create more melodic effects.

Features of Euphony

All euphony examples share the following features:

Euphony involves the use of long vowel sounds, which are more melodious than consonants.

Euphony involves the use of harmonious consonants, such as *l, m, n, r*, and soft *f* and *v* sounds. Euphony uses soft consonants or semi-vowels, including *w, s, y*, and *th* or *wh*, extensively to create pleasant sounds.

English is a strong euphonic language and we have many words whose sounds suit their meaning or whose meaning has come to resemble the sounds. Words like *creepy, eerie, screech* are well, just creepy! Using words with the right euphonic sounds can enhance the meaning in a piece of poetry if you have the message to start with. Adding in random words with euphonic sounds will not in themselves create atmosphere and enhanced understanding.

 Wanting to show fright, unpleasant situations, something off key, the vowel sound of the long *e* is useful. Here we have a few examples. *Fear, squeak, eerie, secret, shriek, weep, creep*. Other words that you can incorporate with the long *e*; *leaf, see, heave.*

Want to emphasise laziness, disinterest? Think of incorporating the consonant *l. Mellow, idle, lazy, languid, lethargic.*

117

The long *oo* sound can add to a dark atmosphere *gloom*, *spook*, *moor*.

Let us explore the sound of the letter *s*. It can add a happy or calm atmosphere in some words such as *suffuse*, *small*, *safe*, *spell*, but equally its sibilance can demonstrate hostility or spitefulness; *hiss*, *slither*, *stink*, so choosing certain sounds with words can change emotion because words have connotations.

This is a very quick introduction to euphony. Go back and consider the long vowels and think about the effects they can potentially have.

There is some thought that the words 'cellar door' are the most beautiful words but recently there has been discussion that this may be a hoax. There are some interesting thoughts on the internet if you care to look for them.

Exercise:

Chose a poem and identify euphony. Look at how the euphonic effects are picked up by other devices that deal in rhyme and repetition.

Exercise:

Go onto the internet and further explore euphony.

Further poetry reading demonstrating Euphony:

Ode to Autumn. John Keats.

Success. Emily Dickinson.

I Have to Tell You. Dorothea Grossman.

Onomatopoeia

At the intersection where noise meets language there are a series of words that are imitations of the sounds they represent. This is called *onomatopoeia*. It is one of the poetic devices related to the use of sound. The formation of a word from a sound associated with an action, object, animal or naturally associated with its properties such as *plop*, *click*, *buzz*, *splat*, *hiss*. These are attempts at imitating a sound. The interesting question is - do these imitations influence the meaning of the other words that they are combined with when we write or talk? Do onomatopoeic words throw up pictures in our minds, send our minds on a chase for other word associations?

In addition to the sounds they represent, many onomatopoeic words have developed meanings of their own. The word *whisper* not only represents the breathiness of people talking quietly but also describes the action of people talking quietly.

These sounds can be grouped in categories. Here are some examples:

119

Human sounds: *gulp, spit, splutter, cough, sniff, sniffle, hiccup, huff, snort, snore, belch*

Hands: *pat, clap, slap, smack*

Animal Sounds:

Dogs: *woof, yip, yap, growl, snarl, howl*

Cats: *meow or miaow, mew, purr*
    Birds: *chirp, cheep, tweet, peep, twitter, crow, squawk*
    Insects: *buzz, chirp, hum*
Engines: *roar, hum, purr*

Horns: *honk, beep*
Exhaust pipes: *sputter, rumble*
Brakes: *squeal, screech*
Explosions: *boom, bang, pop*
Collisions: *crash, bang, clash, wham, smack, whump, thump bump*
 Speed: *zoom, whoosh, swoosh, zing*
Actions: *zip, tap, click*

.

In Act 3 scene 3 of *The Tempest,* Shakespeare used some interesting onomatopoeia. 'A thousand *twangling* instruments'. *Twangling* is a real word; it is a derivative of *twang*. I have got to use it in a poem!

Why do poets use onomatopoeia?

To enhance expressiveness and to evoke the sounds and emotions of real life. To describe things with sounds that are difficult to describe in other ways. As poets we use onomatopoeia to produce rhythm or to produce imagery, it also adds emphasis, has a marked effect on the readers senses and allows the sounds of things to be heard by the reader

With onomatopoeia birds don't just sing sweetly they *trill*, *cheep* or *chirp*. Thawing ice *creaks*, *cracks*. These words and their sounds bring language to life.

Further reading in relation to onomatopoeia.

The Bells. Edgar Allen Poe

I heard a Fly buzz – when I died. Emily Dickinson

Sound repetition; more figurative devices:

For those of you who tend to use rhyme sporadically and prefer unrhymed Free Verse, or for those of you who want to ensure musicality in your verse regardless of the genre you write in, let's look at some of the poetic devices that use sound repetition.

Sounds are the heart of our poetry and how we construct those sounds is our stock in trade.

These types of rhymes (repetitions) are also called *imperfect* or *near* rhymes but they are great devices for use in Free Verse to give musicality.

Assonance

Is the term used to refer to the repetition of a VOWEL SOUND in a line of text or poetry? The words must be close enough together for the repetition to be noticed. Assonance is subtle and is often registered by our 'inner ear'. It is how we subconsciously decide if words work well together.

In Assonance the:

1. vowel sounds are the same

2. consonants after the vowel are not phonetically related

3. the syllables begin differently

In assonance we get tension and partial resolution of sounds.

Why use assonance? You can use it to affect the rhythm tone and mood of your lines.

Examples:

Would you care how long and lonely – repetition of the *o* sound

The light of the fire is a sight. - repetition of the long *i* sound.

Go slow over the road. - repetition of the *o* sound

We light a fire on the mountain. – repetition of the *i* sound

To find assonance rhymes (repetitions) you can use a rhyming dictionary to help you just look under the vowel sound.

If you wanted words you might want to combine in a sentence with *tide* to give assonance, then look up under the long *i* sound.

life, isle, climb, brine, lifeline, survive are some of the options.

Feminine word assonance is even stronger than masculine word assonance.

Assonance in my poem *Tangoing goats*

I can almost see them

hoof to hoof doing

the tango heads thrown

back in romantic abandon

Exercise:

Identify the assonance:

If we meet on street or bus

Say you saw me in the rain

Like a little delicate bird

A strong song gone we decline   Answers p. 363

Further Poetry reading for assonance.

Annabelle Lee by Edgar Allan Poe – long *i*

Tyger by William Blake – long *i*

Daffodils by William Wordsworth. – long *o*

Stopping by the Woods on a Snowy evening by

Robert Frost. – long *o*, long *e*

Consonance

Is the repetition of a CONSONANT SOUND and is typically used to refer to the repetition of sounds at the end of the word, but also refers to repeated sounds in the middle of a word although some people class this type of repetition assonance.

Usually the stressed vowel syllable is in the same position in each word.

In consonance:

1. the syllable sounds are different

2. the consonants after the vowel are the same

3. the syllables begin differently.

Pitter Patter, Pitter Patter - repetition of the *"t,"* and "r" sounds.)

The rent was sent with the tent - repetition of the *"nt"* sound

Gloss the glass boss - repetition of *"ss"*

sin – won -repetition of n sound

save – leave – repetition of the *v* sound

breeze – sneeze – repetition of the *z* sound plus assonance of the long e sound.

He didn't see the lack of thought or care – the repetition of the *ck* of *lack* with the *c* in care. Other words that share consonance using *ck* are *chuckle, fickle, crack, attack.*

These sounds use tension and resolution but only the final consonants make the resolution.

125

Consonance rhyme (repetition) can add emotion to lines; they can be used to underscore emotions. It also gives the feeling of rhyme and the ear picks up the chimes of those repetitions. Consonance is an important tool for the structure of poetry.

Consonance words are easy to find in a rhyming dictionary each vowel sound lists its constant endings alphabetically.

Examples of poems using Consonance

T'was later when the summer went by Emily Dickinson. – repetition of *m* sound.

The Acrobats by Shel Silverstein.

Arms and the Boy by Wilfred Owen.

Alliteration

Is a term to describe a device in which a series of words begin with the same letter or constant sound in adjacent or closely connected words.

Classic examples are:

She sells seashells by the seashore.

Blue and grey black and blue

Every Easter the eggs are painted.

Friendly fire

Dark day's dance

He was devastated when he struck hard luck. - Here you have Alliteration of *was* and *when*, also *struck* and *luck* are perfect rhyme and coincidentally the *k* sound in *ck* is consonance.

Luck and fate were his fall back his excuse. – fate and fall are alliteration.

Alliteration allows the connection of ideas and that sonic repetition that adds musicality. Again, it adds rhythm and flow, highlights ideas and themes and enhances the poetic structure and meaning.

Many companies use alliteration as an easily remembered stand-out name in the marketplace. Alliteration is powerful repetition. Think of all the fictional characters that have alliterative names! Donald Duck, Micky Mouse, Marilyn Monroe.

Further reading alliteration.

***The Rime of the Ancient Mariner* by Samuel Coleridge**

***I know why the caged birds sing* by Maya Angelou**

Serendipitous soliloquy

Does this tirade scan iambically?

I pace the floor while shouting my declamation

Trying to rid myself of my consternation

You swore you loved me, you chased and wooed me

I began to trust and became your devotee

How could I become sucked in to this morass?

I am feeling such an ass.

Can you find other figurative devices in this piece?

Because alliteration gives strong rhythms and definition it can be overdone and if overused it can become boring and switch the reader off. Balance is everything.

Anaphora

Anaphora is the name given to the repetition of a word or words, at the beginning of a sentence, or the beginning of a line, or a clause useful for sonic effects.

Anaphora serves to emphasize certain ideas, which can stir up associated emotions and appeal to the audience in order to inspire, convince or challenge.

128

My life is my purpose. My life is my dream. My life is an obsession.

Everything is full of charm, everything is free from harm, everything is in the scheme.

Martin Luther King Jr.'s speeches and sermons are full of instances of anaphora. For example, his famous *'I Have a Dream'* address.

Further reading of poetry using Anaphora:

Some feel the rain by Joanna Klink.

I see the Body Electric by Walt Whitman.

In music the notes transition one to the other in a smooth harmonious way using small steps often using common tones, these poetic devices using sound allow the poet to make musical chimes and tropes within our poems. Metre is another device using sound to add specific rhythms to poetry. Specifically, it is used with classical poetry forms. Please see the specific chapter on metre towards the end of the book.

Case Study:

I was asked to write a poem based on a work of Art. I
love the work of Alphonse Mucha. He painted Art
Nouveaux theatre posters and pictures so I
chose *Summer Lady* from the Four Seasons.

Lady of Summer.

The epitome of Art Nouveau

Some would say déshabillé

She leans on a bough

eyebrows raised quizzically

as she seems to stare

seductively into the eyes of the viewer

the lady Summer, head bedecked in poppies

feet reflected in a pool of water

seductive alabaster and apricot

I think there is a question

waiting to be asked

She and her twin greet me daily

she graces my bathroom wall

130

of her myriad reincarnations here she

reclines pulling me to an earlier era

She makes me smile

As I close my eyes and become

a representation of

the Lady of Summer and consider her questions

Once I had finished, I put the poem up for critique and it was suggested that whilst the first two lines made a statement, they didn't add anything to the beginning of the poem and might be better moved, so I moved those two lines:

She leans on a bough

eyebrows raised quizzically

as she seems to stare

seductively into the eyes of the viewer

the lady Summer, head bedecked in poppies

feet reflected in a pool of water

seductive alabaster and apricot

131

She and her twin greet me daily

she graces my bathroom wall

of her myriad reincarnations here she

reclines pulling me to an earlier era

She makes me smile

As I close my eyes and become

a representation of

the Lady of Summer

The epitome of Art Nouveau

Some would say déshabillé

This had the effect of opening the poem up and hooks the reader in better. The lines related to questions in stanza one didn't really add anything to the poem, so they were removed. I also tightened up the last lines of stanza 2. This poem is certainly better but after leaving and *rereading the epitome of Art Nouveau* was still not sitting comfortably. Time for another edit:

She leans on a bough

eyebrows raised quizzically

as she seems to stare

seductively into the eyes of the viewer

the lady Summer, head bedecked in poppies

feet reflected in a pool of water

seductive alabaster and apricot

The epitome of Art Nouveau

Some would say déshabillé

She and her twin greet me daily

she graces my bathroom wall

of her myriad reincarnations here she

reclines pulling me to an earlier era

She makes me smile

As I close my eyes and become

a representation of

the Lady of Summer

133

Here is where the poem sits now after three major edits. Poems evolve; we need to change, move, refine our work.

Here you should be able to see the need to read poems carefully after they are written. Read them aloud, listen to them, hear the rhythms, the chimes. Feel how the sound and meaning flow together and if they feel slightly off key, different combinations of words and sounds must be chosen.

Read the three versions, tune into the sound and meaning, picture the lady and her effect on me. Find the sonic devices I have used there are examples of euphony, alliteration, assonance in the poem.

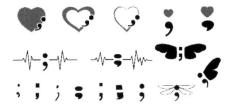

Finding words

When your words flood forth onto the paper, they are the words that immediately come to mind; they are not necessarily the best words you could use. They are the words that flow easily from your brain. Think back to the exercise where you improvised from the first line of a poem. You have a pool of raw language and that now needs to be moulded.

When you have done that first draft of a poem you need to consider:

If your words supply imagery, if they flow, do the sounds of the words you have chosen work well together, do your words have the right connotations for the poem subject and emotion?

We've all read a piece of writing which would stump even the most well-read and linguistically exceptional reader. We've all also read pieces which cause us to wonder if the writer was locked inside a room with a typewriter and reams of paper and a dictionary.

It is easy to grab a thesaurus to find words to describe places and objects in a different manner, but often, the way we speak is also the way we write, so be sure to carefully consider how you want your piece to "sound".

You need to consider your word choice to get just the right effect.

Meaning:

Words can be chosen for either
their denotative meaning, which is the definition
you'd find in a dictionary or the connotative meaning,
which is the emotions, circumstances, or descriptive
variations the word evokes which is important to
enhance mood in the poem.

Level of Diction:

The level of diction an author chooses directly relates
to the intended audience; children will be different to
adults. In poetry it also relates to the poetic device
used, it is better with complex figures of speech to
keep diction simple and straight forward.

Specificity:

Words that are concrete rather than abstract can be
powerful.

It is better to demonstrate abstract words like *love*,
anger with illustrations and instances using similes,
metaphors, personification, giving a concrete picture.

Style:

Word choice is an essential element in the style of any writer. While his or her audience may play a role in the stylistic choices a writer makes, style is the unique voice that sets one writer apart from another.

Sound:

Word choice is all about meaning but it is also all about sound. Poetry is designed for the ear and the eye. The right word will enhance rhythm, the wrong word will destroy it. The right sounds will enhance emotion, enable connections and add reader satisfaction. Be pleasing to the ear.

Remember, your work will be judged on your word choices and how well you utilise the words at your disposal.

One of the best methods for ensuring that you pick the correct word for what you want to convey is to read. Read the "great" Classical poets and the modern ones, too. See how they craft their pieces, what words they chose, and try to figure out why they chose the words they did. Sylvia Plath, Charles Bukowski, Robert Frost, Carl Sandburg, and Allen Ginsberg were masterful in their word choices. Jim Morrison was an exceptional poet, and all of the Renaissance poets. Read their work, digest their words, and let

137

your pen fly with confidence that you too, will become masterful in your word choices.

Pointers for choosing words

Choose words that are likely to work with your audience.

Use precise words, be comfortable with the words you use.

Choose strong verbs as this limits unnecessary adverbs and adjectives.

Avoid overused or clichéd words.

Avoid obsolete words or archaic words.

Check connotations and synonyms.

Check for overuse of adjectives.

Choose words that complement each other.

Consider the sound of the words and the letters; do they add musicality to the line?

Exercise:

Read the following poem and see what you think about the use of language.

Agog, I am supine

Enamoured of your munificence

I live in ethereal solitude

From whence you emerged

Bequeathing amorous bouquets

Of unrequited love

On vellum, parched parchment puzzles

And diversions direct us

Hearken, you lowly worms of insignificancies

Your empress, and matriarch beguiles herself

Bow and scrape before her travesties,

Prostrate yourself before her magnificence

For you know not where your future lies

Take the panacea; imbibe your elixir

So that you become as I am inured

Soulless, sullen and enamoured

Stay strong and focused

So that we may adore her

Forever.

By Eric Keizer (written for this exercise)

Heavy? Too obscure? Believe me, I have seen poems written like this, but I have rarely persevered to the end, I enjoy interacting with a poem but there are limits!

Exercise:

Rewrite the poem with words that convey the meaning in an easy to digest form.   Example on p 363

Words, the poet's stock in trade, shouldn't just be plucked from the head but should be chosen with care. The poet might start with a poem that grows out of a stream of consciousness but then those words need pruning and polishing. Think about connotations that can associate the word to other meanings that can act to subliminally influence the reader. Be clear in understanding the meanings of words and references. Always look up any words you do not regularly use, or which are used in unfamiliar ways.

Consider the etymologies. Sometimes the root of the word can be used to make interesting connections.

Avoid words that are archaic or inappropriate. Avoid using a word that isn't needed just to make a rhyme. The use of any slang words, innuendoes, puns, ambiguities should be fully intended and not accidental.

In *Only the sea shall Change,* Andrew Neil Carpenter has chosen his words with care to get rhyme and rhythm, chime and musicality. His use of the repetition of *s* along the lines, the *z* in *breeze* and *wheeze* also adds to the *s* sound. The repetition of the *e* sound enhances the musicality and helps to paint pictures we can see.

With endless wheeze, the saline breeze

Displeases all who wander on

The dunes, the beach, both leached and bleached

By jagged winds of sharp contour.

But just one man is swayed to stay,

In *Silence of the Birds* (see p.25) my word choice was important. I used *water colour painting* then removed the word *painting* as the idea of watercolour was a metaphor. I wanted to show an early morning in spring, cool, with the sun emerging but the air misty. Again, the use of the *s* sound in the words *suffused, standing, stark, small, shoreline, sky* adds a harmonious atmosphere to a poem. The use of the short *i* adds musicality. The internal rhyme of *stark* and *dark* add tension and resolution to the lines.

141

Consider David John Terelinck's choice of words below from *Armistice*. He is describing an unhappy couple and he's using the picture of food residue to describe the feelings of a leftover argument. David has chosen words related to conflict and he has emphasised the movement through his short stanzas by his use of several words utilising **L**. *L* has connotations of languid motion of things slowly moving forward which is just what events in this poem are doing. Again, we have the **S** sound but this time the choice of the *s* sound is to bring unease. The repeat of c sounds and the short *i*.

Lips pursed, leftovers

from last night's argument still cling

 to the corners of your mouth.

Spilled milk and breadcrumbs,

war crimes of domesticity,

destroy the ceasefire of irritable

silence.

David DB Hall has chosen interestingly contrasting words here: *'crisply sneaking'.*

Autumn dusk can be so seductive

crisply sneaking in

unawares of the clock's pointy hands

erasing the day's heat.

"I was wanting to use words to indicate that first nip of fall's cool air sneaking in at dusk after the heat of those dog days of summer." David DB Hall.

This is great imagery with a small sketch where we can all visualise the scene. Note sounds can evoke so many emotions and therefore the choice of words and the letters that make them up are of real importance to the poet. Using the right musical sounds really facilitates the best emotions.

The order of words

The order of the words used in a line is also important and here we are thinking about line structure. There are two ways that the sentence can be constructed, and this is either in an active or a passive voice.

In the active voice the subject is the doer of the action

143

In the passive voice the action is done to the subject

Here are two examples:

John read the student's poetry (active)

The student's poetry was read by John (passive)

Billy wore a hat (active)

A hat was worn by Billy (passive)

For poetry the active voice is what we are looking for. Sometimes inverting the syntax to engage with a rhyme will cause the sentence to be passive.

Word Inversion.

Where possible in modern poetry words shouldn't be inverted changing them from normal speech to that more suited to Yoda from Star Wars. Whilst Shakespeare and poets in the 18th century regularly wrote lines that today have an archaic syntax, this was poetry of their time. Inversion is also called *anapostrophe*.

Inversion is achieved by doing the following:

Placing an adjective after the noun it qualifies - *the man strong*

Placing a verb before its subject - *shouts the policeman*

144

In English there are inversions that are part of grammar structure and are quite common in their use. For instance, inversion always occurs in interrogative statements where verbs, or auxiliaries, or helping verbs are placed before their subjects. Similarly, inversion happens in typical exclamatory sentences where objects are placed before their verbs and subjects, and preceded by a *wh-* word, such as the following examples of inversion:

What a beautiful garden it is!

Where in the world were you?

How wonderful the weather is today!

These are fine in speech and in prose but use with care in poetry.

If you are rhyming do not say:

To the shop I will go.

The sea blue.

Agree with you the teacher does.

Or any other such sense twisting it can be irksome in modern poetry. Unless you are writing a total imitation of Shakespeare don't use language in the same way he did.

145

Keep Thinking about sounds and words.

Find the Assonance in the following:

The murky brown fog rolled over the Downs.

Look at your shadow striding behind you.

Find assonance rhymes to fill in the blanks.:

- Hang onto ….
- I spilt the milk …..

Find Consonance rhymes in the following:

Torch. Forgiven, love, phrase.

Find the alliteration in this:

The ship hove to as rising waves crashed down

White foam flecks the air as howling

Winds blows the water into a frenzied attack.

Selecting words – Concrete and Abstract Word choice

Concrete words and imagery versus abstractions.

The ability to write a poem that is vivid and has a picture a reader can paint is down to the use of concrete words and imagery.

Why, oh why, did anyone label using the literal meaning of words concrete. As a concept it makes many people's eyes glaze.

The choice of concrete and abstract words and images is important in poetry. This choice is the basis of imagery, necessary for writing effective metaphors and similes.

Go on to Facebook and read poems on some of the poetry sites and you will see there will be a lot of words dedicated to telling the reader how they should feel, or huge swathes devoted to feelings, usually complex, abstract feelings.

Poets want to be poetic and they think a way to do it is to disclaim emotions and use lots of large abstract words to get their message across. Fine, great, but is that what the reader wants? Is it what the reader remembers?

If you stop and think about the moments in stories and poems that have really made an impact, you are probably thinking of very specific images.

You are probably not thinking of a description--no matter how flowery-- of feelings. *"I was really really really happy. I mean way happy. I was the happiest."*

 It will be the gentle touch of a soothing hand, the heart wrenching moment that and incident happened.

Abstract words

Abstract ideas are words that you can't measure with your senses; you can't hold, touch, see smell or taste them. They are also ideas that change; that are not static. If you take *happiness*, it's a nebulous feeling. Eating a donut may cause happiness, winning lots of money may cause happiness, having survived an accident may cause happiness, the completion of a poem may cause happiness. These feelings will vary in intensity, we know the person is feeling good in some way. In some circumstances that is enough, but we would react more strongly if we had a stronger understanding of happiness in the context in which it's being used.

But you can't put happiness in a jar; you can't buy a pound of it; you can't weigh it. The reader has experience of happiness from their own lives and this is the only way they can view the abstract idea.

Freedom, another abstract word. Free to do what I want with no restrictions, freedom from prison, escape from a too tight waist band, a paid holiday, the ability to make my own decisions so what does freedom look like, mean, smell like in the context of a poem?

With abstract words *friendly, democracy, horror, joy, misery* we think we understand them, but we only understand them in the context of our experience and our understanding and there is more than one understanding; there are many.

Therefore, the poet needs to add context to the abstractions usually by describing it in concrete terms or adding some sort of concrete imagery to ground the idea.

Concrete words

These are words that you can measure with the senses you can see, hear, touch, taste or smell them; they are literal.

This is directly opposite to abstract terms, which name things that are not available to the senses. Concrete terms include *spoon, table, velvet, red, hot, walk, bread, water, ice.* Because these terms refer to objects or events we can see or hear or feel or taste or

149

smell, their meanings are stable. If you ask me what I mean by the word spoon, I can pick up a spoon and show it to you. I can describe it to you, yes there are different types of spoon, but we can all visualise a spoon and what it does. I can weigh potatoes, smell gas but I can't pour beauty into a jug or point out a small amount of anger crawling on the floor. While abstract terms will change at different times in your life and in different circumstances, *dog, water, run* keep static meanings through one's life.

You may think you understand and agree with me when I say, "We all want affluence". But surely, we don't all want the same things. Affluence means different things to each of us, and you can't be sure of what I mean by that abstract term. If I say, "I want a six bedroomed mansion and a Ferrari in my driveway", you know exactly what I mean, and you know whether you want the same things or different things. The concrete terms are clearer and give you more context than abstract terms.

Does this mean we shouldn't use abstract terms in poetry? No - as with everything we need a balance. Sometimes we need abstract terms. We need to use ideas and concepts, and we need terms that represent them. But we must understand how imprecise their meanings are, how easily they are misunderstood, and how boring chains of abstract terms can be. Abstract terms are useful and necessary when we want to name ideas but they're not likely to make points clear or interesting by themselves.

If you think about moments from books, films or poems that have stayed with you. It's probably not going to be something like this:

Sweeter than scoops of ice-cream, were some days

Bitter than coffee grounds, were few nights,

Erratic is life, and so are its varying flavours

Nevertheless, life must be led with all our might.

It's more likely to be specific concrete imagery:

I was confronted with a huge sense of loss. I felt empty, weak, so miserable.

I touch the open half read book on the table besides his chair, he will never finish it now.

My hands shake as I clear the second-place setting, I had automatically set.

I will never lay my head on his shoulder and smell Brut in the space next to his neck.

151

No one would suggest that a writer can never talk about feelings, but the way to do so is to ground those feelings in concrete details. A writer who wants to delve into abstractions will have to work much harder to earn that moment. Humans don't think in abstractions. We think in concrete sensory details.

Here is the first Version of my poem *Duality*. I am on to Version 4.

Duality

My Love feels like
I am   wrapped
in a warm fluffy blanket
Safe, sheltered, succoured
yet it can be like
an icy draft stinging my eyes,
Adding goosebumps to my skin,
the chill when the blanket slips.

My love tastes like
Smooth and mellow chocolate
Sweet and melting   on the tongue,
*leaving a feeling of **contentment***
Sometimes it has the sharp tart taste of lemon
or the crisp nuttiness of almonds
tastes to savour and linger over
it can taste like

152

Pepper, mustard and vinegar mixed
harsh on the tongue   bad for the stomach
Sometimes it tastes of chilli and spice – heat
that travels across by skin making
my skin sheen in perspiration and
my nerve ends tingle.

Love is abstract but I am explaining it with concrete examples. Some abstract words slipped in as they do!

Did I need

"Safe, sheltered, succoured"?

The reader should be able to nuance these feelings from their experience of a warm fluffy blanket, without being told and they are all abstract words. *"leaving a feeling of contentment"* This is telling with the use of contentment. Most people would appreciate that chocolate melting on the tongue is a pleasant feeling that would lend to feelings of contentment. Again, contentment is abstract. Or if I wanted to keep *contented* in, I could amend those lines - *my love is a contented tongue tasting smooth mellow chocolate* - Now making a metaphor.

We will revisit the use of concrete and abstract words in the chapters on imagery, sense bound writing and figurative language.

Start to think of the abstract words you and others use and how you gauge the meaning of what people are saying. Think of the word bad so many connotations.

If somebody says the food is bad how do you differentiate between food that tastes unpleasant or is of poor quality or is literally rancid and dangerous?

When somebody says that was a really bad movie do, they mean it was boring? The acting was poor? Are they being ironic and mean it was quite good? It could be around the choice of descriptors; it could be related to nonverbal cues and tone of voice. In writing we only have the words we use and the emotions we can create when we use words and sound together. The vaguer we are in our use of abstract terms the more the reader will populate the story with their own viewpoint without the support of a strong structure from the poet.

Selecting Words – Verbs, Adjectives and Adverbs

Selecting the right words can make a huge difference to how your poem reads. With language being concentrated and the word count limited you need to remove excess words and check your words carefully.

Using excess words can be a problem if you add in extra verbs, adjectives or adverbs to qualify emotion or action. These describing and intensifying words also 'tell'. Sometimes though the unqualified expression is the strongest. *I love you very much* is fine, but *I love you* is the stronger statement.

Using abstract words pushes the reader away from the action when they need to be immersed in it, seeing what the narrator is seeing, feeling what the narrator is feeling. The reader needs to be able to use all their senses and their experience of life to get a rich picture.

She looked at him he *seemed sad.*

Seemed? Sad?

I want to know how the poet visualises this; is it slightly sad, or mildly disturbed, or devastated?

He pointed a shaking finger at his house, tears streaming down his face.

This gives you a better feeling for the degree of sadness he was feeling no need to say sad a better picture. Yes, I have chosen more words in this example to illustrate the point. In a poem I may well use more words, but they will be chosen for purpose, not just the statement of unadorned emotion. Or I may be able to whittle the words down or use different words if it was a line in a poem.

Here's a list of words for you to watch out for that may not always add benefit to your lines:

- to see
- to hear
- to think
- to touch
- to wonder
- to realize
- to watch
- to look
- to seem
- to feel (or feel like)
- can
- to decide
- to sound (or sound like)
- to notice
- to be able to

- to note
- to experience
- emotion words. love, anger, pain, sad,
- adjectives such as beautiful, sexy
- abstract words like freedom

Let us look at a couple of examples of lines with extra words that add no benefit:

I see the balloon rise overhead.
The balloon rises overhead.

He watched her dance in the rain.
She danced in the rain.

Both mean exactly the same and the *I see,* and *he watched* are irrelevant to understanding.

Every word in poetry needs to be necessary to enhance meaning or emotion.

There is a place for these words and phrases, but they should act as **red flags** in your writing, when you edit, check if using the word is the best way to write an image.

Use active verbs.

It was cold.
She breathed into her hands to warm her numb
fingers.

Tina felt tired.
She rubbed her eyes.

Samantha seemed impressed.
Samantha's eyes widened, and her lips formed a
silent, "Wow!"

Samantha looked as if she was going to cry.
Samantha's bottom lip started to quiver.

Can you see the difference? The passive sentence is
just telling a reader what is happening, the active
sentence shows the reader.

**Here is another issue with the use of verbs and
sound.**

Look at the lines and read aloud.

life devoid of excitement
her need making her reckless

life devoid of excitement
her need makes her reckless

Two lines from a poem using "*making*"; if you use "*makes*" it forces a fundamental change on the sound of that line. If you read both versions, aloud, slowly. There is a sonic effect in the second line that does not occur in the first version, can you identify it? When you read it aloud can you detect the caesura between "*makes*" and "*her*"? This is not there between "*making*" and "*her*". This is what accentuates the rhythm and can be used to accent the poem. It is one of the reasons to avoid using "*ing*" verbs and to move to the base form of the verb. It also removes unintended chimes from the poem and puts more emphasis on the more subtle use of other sonic devices. This is as important, but in a more subtle way as using rhyme well.

But importantly, using the base form of the verb makes the event more immediate and focuses on the moment.

Adjectives and Adverbs

An adjective is a part of speech that describes and modifies a noun, to make a writing or conversation more specific, relevant, and coherent. The word "adjective" has been derived from the Latin word *adjectivum*, which means "additional."

An adverb is a part of speech that provides greater description to a verb, adjective, another adverb, a phrase, a clause, or a sentence. A great way to pick out an adverb from a sentence is to look for the word ending in *-ly*.

Adverbs are intensifiers and they can even come in the form of an adverb phrase.

Poetry requires good imagery and adjectives add detail to nouns, adverbs too add description and intensities so one would expect poetry to be liberally sprinkled with each. The issue is the sparsity of words in poetry, the concentration of language.

In some ways that means to make poetry evocative layering adverbs and adjectives into lines is the quickest way to great imagery.

However, adjectives and adverbs if overused can tip the poem over the edge into purple prose. The piece is over poetic but not good poetry. If you consider the adverb, using an adverb to mitigate the effect of a verb usually means that you may be using the wrong verb. Fine in prose, but it is an extra word or two in a poem, and if we want to get the right words in the right order then adverbs point to an issue with the verb. Take the phrase, *"he walked slowly along the road"*. This could be *"he meandered along the road", "he strolled along the road", "he crept along the road".* You get the picture, or maybe the picture is too vague, like the word maybe. The verb can be chosen more carefully to underline the tone you want to get into the poem. To a certain extent the same is true of the adjectives, but here it is a case of using only the most effective adjectives to mitigate the noun and therefore to ensure that it is not too much. Here is an example of one of my poems. The first normal, the second with adjectives and adverbs removed , and the third with just the most essential adjectives. Think about which of the poems works best.

My poems:

1.   Surrounded by love as he sits in his chair
he feels the warm glow of affection
Yet there is a chill in the air
One only he can feel like an iced laced dart
Pushing through his defenses and into his heart
Keeping him on edge and reminding him of past
times
He knows that the mask he wears hides
hideous crimes

Yet he knows the veneer is so fragile, and thin
It could shatter and then his demons would win
His shady past life sits like a crown of thorns
Wrapping his heart in chains that are
Tainted by the devil's horns

Watching the smiling faces
Filled with love and with trust
His guilt a burden under whose weight
he is crushed.

2.   Surrounded by love he sits in his chair
he feels the glow of affection.
a chill in the air
One he can feel a dart
Pushing his defenses and into his heart
Keeping him on edge Reminding him of times

162

That the mask he wears hides crimes
He knows the veneer is and
It could shatter -his demons could win
His life sits a crown of thorns
Wrapping his heart in chains
Tainted by the devil's horns
Watching the smiling faces
Filled with love and trust
His guilt a burden
from the weight, he is crushed
3.
Surrounded by love
He sits in his chair
He feels the warmth of affection.
Yet a chill in the air
One he can feel just like
an iced laced dart
Pushing through his defenses
Into his heart
It keeps him on edge
Reminds him that
the mask he wears
hides his horrible crimes

He knows the veneer is
so fragile, and thin
It could shatter then his
hidden demons   might win
His past life sits a crown of thorns

163

Wrapping his heart in chains
Tainted by the devil's horns
He watches their smiling faces
Filled with love and trust
His guilt a burden
from the heavy weight, he is crushed.

Adjectives?? I am in Love. 1

Punctuation in Poetry

In poetry punctuation comes with experience and understanding. Often sense and meaning stretch over more than one line and so the comma gets used as a pause for breath between thoughts or clauses, they can be used to alter rhythm separate consecutive ideas. Commas should be used with purpose not sprinkled randomly at the end of lines. Semi colons are trickier and are seen less often in poetry they are a means to give a stronger pause to join thoughts that would not work well if joined with a comma. The full stop acts much as in prose. Some poets favour the em dash it is used to replace commas, give emphasis to indicate a change in thought.

Why then are many modern poets eschewing those rules? Lines do not start with a capital letter; line stops, and pauses are demonstrated just by the end of lines and white space. Questions are read by the reader with their own emphasis recognising a question by the usage of words. Is it because poets are rebels and don't like to follow the rules? Or is it about taking risks for the sake of art or for the sake of a piece?

Many poets have successfully skirted grammar rules and produced great poems, others have not. Others have used grammar rules badly which equally ruins the reading of the poem.

165

The thing to remember; whichever style you choose it needs to be done well.

Going down a *no punctuation* or *partial punctuation* route in modern poetry does not mean that poor spelling is acceptable or lazy writing where prepositions and conjunctions are removed or added arbitrarily straining the meaning of lines.

Whatever you do needs to be consistent, so the reader understands that this style is a part of your poem and not just annoying uncorrected mistakes.

Not using punctuation can mean working harder and getting your poem to have perfect balance, flow and sense. Using punctuation means getting it right.

If you choose to forgo the rules because you don't know them rather than as a creative technique, your lack of knowledge will show, and the poem will present as amateurish. Of course, that's true for all types of writing: learn the rules, and only after you have learned them, go ahead and break them.

I salute anyone who breaks the rules in the interest of art and great poetry writing just as much as I admire poets who craft meter and verse within the confines of grammar. For me, either way is the right way. In the reading sections you have seen poems that use punctuation and some that do not.

What are your thoughts on applying punctuation rules to poetry writing? Are you a stickler for good punctuation, even in your creative or experimental work, or do you like to bend and break the rules?

Patterns and Repetitions in Poetry

Repetition is about returning to a theme, a word or a musical sounding phrase. If you are using repetition in your poetry, it is important that you are using it consciously and for a reason. You should use it intentionally to make a point, build a rhythm or create a feeling.

You can repeat individual words to create emphasis on that word, or whole phrases or refrains.

Have you thought about how poems have repetitions in a way that prose doesn't? That the aural, visual aspects are gathered in patterns. How that affects the structure of poetry?

Repetition of a sound, syllable, word, phrase, line, stanza, or metrical pattern is a basic unifying device. It may reinforce, supplement, or even substitute for metre or rhythm.

Poetry was traditionally concerned with the sounds and meaning of the words, but as a written medium, we cannot deny that there is also a presentation on the page, and that the patterns developed in that visual field can't be overlooked if we are to concern ourselves with the full potential of the poem's structure. We have already explored lines, stanzas, white space so you should have a feel for patterning visually.

167

Aural patterns in a poem are concerned largely with the rhythm, sound and tone of the words and letters; how they sound when read in time. Visual pattern and variation are geared more toward the poem's placement on the page than in the way it sounds when read. More concerned with how the words look when revealed in space.

We pick up repetitions by reading the words on the page but if poetry is read aloud the sounds of patterns will be very clear.

We can see and hear the arrangement into repetitive forms, which create structure in a poem. Recurring aspects of written language are letters, diphthongs, words, phrases, lines.

Recurrence and predictability are the basis of pattern. This is what our brain's look for in every aspect of our lives, patterns and order. The poet can exploit the brains longing for order by working on patterns within their poetry.

Verbal: A verbal pattern derives from word choice. Verbal patterns arise in the common letter configurations and repetition of certain words. The exact repetition of words in the same metrical pattern at regular intervals often forms a refrain, which adds stability or indicates shifts or developments of emotion. Such repetitions may serve as commentary, a static point against which the rest of the poem develops, or it may simply be a pleasing sound pattern to fill out a form. Repetition of a word or phrase at the beginning of a set of lines, clauses or phrases (anaphora).

As a unifying device repetition is found extensively in free verse, repetition of a grammar pattern reinforced by the recurrence of actual words and phrases governs the rhythm which helps to distinguish free verse from prose. Repetition of consonant sounds at the start of stressed syllables (alliteration), repetition of vowel sounds in close proximity (assonance), repetition of consonant sounds in the middle or the ends of words (consonance).

Exercise:

Here is Susannah Bailey's *Going Home.* Work your way through the visual repetitions.

Start with the recurrence of words in the poem, these can easily be scanned and seen. Since a poem has some qualities that are unique only to poetry, namely line and stanza, they are also possible places to seek repetition and subsequently pattern.

169

With brief enthusiasms, little more than verbal spasms

The guard shouts 'all aboard the (muffled) train'

'And the next stop is (inaudible again)'

A baby howls, my neighbour scowls

Exhaling cheese and onion

Cheese and onion

Cheese and onion

The fields, hamlets, lowering sky,

Graffitied bridges and hedges fly

We rattle along to my favourite place

And I am leaving London

Leaving London

Leaving London

Suddenly we're in reverse

Something is strange and rather perverse

I may be wrong, but this doesn't seem right

I hear thud thud not clackety clack

Clackety clack

Clackety clack.

Let's look at the first two stanzas:

In stanza 1 there is the repetition of *cheese* and *onion* three times.

In stanza 2 the repetition of *leaving London.*

There are several repetitions of the letter *s* inside words and at the beginning and end. Did you notice the repetition of *a* sounds? You have the repetition of the sound of stressed syllables which will give you rhyme -*train, again, fly, sky, howls, scowls.*

All lines start with capitals, none of the lines have punctuation at the end, there is a small amount of comma use to indicate a pause between words. There is repetition of line length in the last two lines of each stanza. Can you find grammatical repetition, other sound repetition within the piece?

This poem is about being on a train and those repetitions at the end of each stanza give you the sound of a train running on a track.

You can also use repetition to create a circular story by beginning and ending the poem with the same line.

Like a painter at a canvas, the poet looks at how the poem sits on the white canvas of the blank page and how that visual structure creates patterns that can be used to create a richer poem. As a musician or composer, the poet coordinates the words, spaces, punctuation and grammar to ensure the repetitions and harmonisation of the sounds of poems to make them rich and alive.

Imagery in Poetry

In poetry, *Imagery* refers to an author's use of vivid and descriptive language to add depth to writing. Imagery allows the poet to create visual representations of ideas in the readers' minds. It also helps the readers to understand the concept better and relate using their own experiences to enrich the picture.

An image is not the true world although that is its source. It is that impression/translation of the world in our minds. Once in our minds the pictures of flower garden, the crunch of feet on gravel, the coldness of the ocean when we paddle, spilled paint on the floor are stored and we can retrieve them and send them out again but transformed by our interpretation.

Images can be simple or complex, but our brains look for detail. We gauge the event in many ways; perception, identification, comparison, patterning, emotion - liking/disliking, threat, use of memory all building the image in our minds. Images in our minds become facts and are stored in different ways. If we wish to show those facts our 'seeing', to others, they will be retrieved in a variety of forms - literal description, statements, questions, narrative, suppositions, similes, metaphors.

The amazing thing about our minds is that they are never still; always working, turning over ideas, images, testing the contents of our library making new connections in our subconscious. Musing?

The poet takes those concepts, incidents, pictures, stories stored in their minds and translates them in words, sounds and emotions into new imagery for their readers. That is your challenge, poets, to translate your view of an event into imagery that a reader can relate to and they magically transform into an image or concept.

How do we explain the difference between an effective poem and one that fails to grab the reader?

By the effectiveness of its imagery – and the strength and effectiveness of that imagery relies on its concreteness. In fact, real imagery can't help but be concrete.

Despite "image" being a synonym for "picture", images need not be only visual; any of the senses (sight, hearing, touch, taste, smell, motion, internal sensation) can be the key to the imagery that a poet writes.

Visual imagery composed of elements related to sight. It has the capability to paint an actual image (scene or event) in a reader's mind.

Auditory imagery; hearing related. It is the effective use of words that give a sense of sound. Onomatopoeia plays a large role in auditory imagery with the use of words that are close to their actual familiar sound, for example, *bang, pop, boom*, and so on.

Olfactory imagery concerned with the sense of smell. It describes specific scents, for example fruit or food, that help the reader envisage this sense.

Gustatory imagery relies on the use of imagistic words and line construction to impart a sense of taste.

Tactile imagery relies on word choice that depicts touch and sensation.

Kinaesthetic imagery is that which shows movement of people or objects. It is the most active of all the imagery in a poem.

Organic imagery is one of the most difficult to employ. It is tasked with arousing internal emotion in the reader, without using actual emotive words. It is imagery that can evoke elation, fear, sadness, grief,

175

anger and loss, without employing those specific terms

Here you are retranslating all the imagery in your mind from the mixing pot of your 'musing'.

Examples of non-visual imagery can be found in Andrew Neil Carpenter's **Only the sea shall change**:

With endless wheeze, the saline breeze

Displeases all who wander on

Here we have sound in the *wheezy breeze* (can't you just hear it?) and smell the *saline breeze*.

In **Jacaranda Blue on Blue** Laurie Grove has also used sound and the wind to create a different mechanism, to create a soothing effect:

The southern wind lullaby's

Through my branches; it sings:

*In **Potential** I have used Taste imagery and Organic imagery:*

Let us distill each drop of emotion

Make us taste both bitterness and sweetness

176

In **Music at Dusk,** David DB Hall has used
kinaesthetic imagery, organic imagery and sound:

*Stretching reclinered limbs, catching breath with
forgotten lungs.*

Over-worked people emerge

from their social media slumber

stretching reclinered limbs

to the tune of rice krispies

catching breaths with forgotten lungs

eyes adjusting from apple screens.

In **Music at Dusk,** David DB Hall also used tactile
imagery:

Bodies anchored by gravity of excess

bare feet caressed by fresh cut grass

In **Jacaranda Blue on Blue,** Laurie Grove has used
Tactile Imagery as well:

*Many arms wrap themselves round my old gnarled
skin.*

To the weary; many arms

Wrap themselves round

177

My old gnarled skin,

And many tears nourish

The sap in my veins.

Here I was asked to describe a bed using imagery and as many senses as possible

It's a self-effacing bed, despite its size

like two football pitches

it likes to dress simply in plain colours

although it insists on being covered in a duvet

it likes a light one in summer

then a warm thick duvet in winter

it likes the weight of pillows on its head

and keeps them perched ready for me

it is soft and sprung and I can snuggle

into it and it cradles me until I go to sleep

as I breathe deep, I smell soap and spring flowers

the sheets feel cool and soft as I turn

over to get more comfortable

the bed sighs at being treated as a trampoline

178

and shakes me gently, my bed is so alluring

I think it would taste like a chocolate covered

marshmallow as I sink into its

gooey sweetness transported on the Happy

magic carpet of dreams.

How many senses can you identify?

There are so many ways poets can simply tell us things but that leaves out context and depth. A poet could simply state, *I see the sea,* but it is possible to conjure up a much more specific image using techniques such as **simile** (*the sea like a wrinkled blanket, the sea is like a revolving drum, the sea like a rabid dog),* or **metaphor** *(an azure cloth drying on a line, a grey juggernaut exceeding the speed limit)* or **synecdoche** *(white capped waves)* - each of these suggests a different kind of sea, different conditions. Techniques, such as these, that can be used to create powerful images use figurative language, and can include onomatopoeia, metonymy and personification.

179

One of the great pleasures of poetry is discovering particularly powerful images that enhance the poems story.

Look at this fabulous piece of imagery by Laurie Grove.

She soars snowdrift and rockslide,
Over Puno down to Lake Titicaca,
Clipping the waves,
Wind foam in her crest,
As Cassiopeia dances off
The dark mirrored surface;
Feathers brushing the sand
Along the shoreline, in search
Of carrion to carry home,

Can you picture the soaring bird? The geography? Go back and reread *Divine Amazon* (p. 31) and visualise that Condor in flight over her South American home.

Writing using the senses

When a poem stimulates and provokes the senses, as you read you draw on images from your own experiences. You shape the images from your mind. They involve you, so the poem becomes about you or at the very least you are riding firmly with the narrator, experiencing what they are, but from your understanding of the world. That's the power of sense-bound writing. It pulls the reader into the poem by using their own experiences as part of the poem's material. We looked at the description of sense bound imagery in the previous chapter. Make it a part of your writing routine.

I always have a note beside me as I write to remind me to include sense generated imagery in my poetry.

sight

hearing

smell

taste

touch

motion

emotion/ internal feelings

181

Exercise: Read this stanza:

With brief enthusiasms, little more than verbal
spasms
The guard shouts 'all aboard the (muffled) train'
'And the next stop is (inaudible again)'
A baby howls, my neighbour scowls
Exhaling cheese and onion
Cheese and onion
Cheese and onion

Where do these words take you? Do they make you
see something? A train? Can you hear the guard on
the tannoy, gargling, giving inaudible information?
Can you hear the echo of the train in the repetitions
giving the train wheel rhythm? Can you picture a
railway carriage is it full? empty? Is it going to be a
comfortable journey do you think?

Now consider these lines:

Press a button to add a soundtrack
the gentle rustling, swooshing of the grass
the slap flap of jackets moving in the breeze
overlaid by the distinctive boom boom of the Bittern.

What are you experiencing when you read this poem?

182

Can you visualise the scene? Hear the wind, the sounds. Will they be the same as mine? Probably not, but hopefully a sound of wind making grass scratch, vibrate, rattle will come to your mind. You may never have heard a Bittern call but those onomatopoeic words *boom boom* will help you hear their resonating call.

Whether they are the same pictures or different, hopefully those words will have painted some pictures in your mind; rustling grass, the sound of clothes moving in a wind or even if only the smell of cheese and onion crisps! In both the poems the poets have used sense-bound writing to show the reader what is unfolding rather than telling them.

Here is a piece of sense-bound writing I did for a challenge:

The slow sound of bass notes entwined

with the trailing notes of violins, rise in the air

as I bite into the peach tasting the sweetness

of honey, the aroma full of complex pheromones

like your aftershave, I shudder as my paisley shawl

slips across my skin.

I tried to include several senses; can you identify them?

Good poetry is loaded with imagery mostly generated using senses. As Anton Chekhov commented about the art of showing *"Don't tell me the moon is shining; show me the glint of light on broken glass."*

Using the senses in writing poetry will always pull the reader into the piece; it enables the reader to experience the poem beside the narrator.

The opening lines and stanza of a poem are the first chance a poet gets to hook the reader. The initial opportunity for the poet to say *"Come. Hold my hand. Take this journey with me"*. If you don't hook the reader with your opening, will they stay the distance with your poem? With that in mind, would the following lines encourage you to read on? Do they capture your interest? Are they enticing? Do you want to hang around to find out what comes after? Does it set a scene you would like to know more about? Do you like these opening lines . . . why, or why not?

"Warm pale rays,

the colour of just-ripe quinces,"

David John Terelinck.

Consciousness bound writing

Writing good effective imagery is imperative for good poetry. It's not always easy to show imagery and so it's good to practice this skill. A good way to do this is by practicing *stream of consciousness* writing or pulling an idea down to base level. Object writing describing an object, a place, or a feeling.

Here is something poets should do every day to really develop depth of imagery and make sense-bound writing as natural as breathing. Sit down to write on a subject for a fixed time period - 2 to 8 minutes each day; vary the amount of time. Doing this allows you to use the senses and pull out images. This is about letting the consciousness flow freely, not about beautiful flowing writing. Write, don't think, or labour the writing. You can jot down notes or sentences. In this form of exercise, you are just interested in what ideas might spill and what images might be made.

Here are two pieces I did about autumn:

Colours red and gold, change to brown. Leaf drop, drifts of leaves. Season of apples. Chestnuts spikey shells smooth polished brown nuts like highly polished mushroom caps. Mist like a veil over the countryside. Morning dew heavy on the grass

185

*sparkling in the low sun. Spiders webs bedecked by
sparkling water droplets. Strength of the web
anchorage points. Trap. Larder. The spiders web a
trampoline trap. Spiders web is a lit helicopter
platform on an oil rig. Abseiling spiders. Every year,
the autumnal cycle.*

*Autumn opens the door and sets out the ingredients
for her recipe she has a cornucopia of treats. In
preparation for winter. Each year a different
combination of ingredients mixed in new ways
depending on the gifts left from summer. Her palate
of colours red, brown, gold, yellow the colour of
beauty. Yet dwindling to the browns and blacks of
decay. Autumn encourages trees and bushes to reuse
their nutrients until the colour is leached and they
fall in swathes. Autumn stirs the life of each coloured
leaf and sweeps the corpses into pyramids of sound
and movement. Leaves get kicked up by autumn wind
often vicious and violent resentful of the passing of
summer days. Morning frosts ice branches and as
they walk people's breath puffs like wraiths from
their lips . Black footsteps on the dew spangled grass.
I pause by the hedge and pick a ripe blackberry,
globular glistening and succulent my mind
anticipates the taste as I pop it in my mouth. Sweet
with a hint of sourness like a sugared lemon. Then
the bitter after taste of crunched seeds.*

186

Why should you make this short exercise part of your routine?

This makes writing within you a habit, it enables you to dive deeply into sense-bound writing. You go where your writing takes you, you don't have to rein in your imagination or stay on subject; this is pure, free style. You will find that after the first few attempts you will be immersed in your writing when your timed session finishes but try to stop. This may frustrate the writer within, but it will also keep writing and ideas bubbling in your brain during the day. The next time you do the exercise you will write faster be open to more possibilities which will help you in writing specific poetry and you will also have material, to utilise in your poetry. Material for new imagery and metaphors.

Exercise:

Identify the senses used in that piece of timed writing. Could you pick elements of the piece to make the basis of a poem?

If so, why not try.

Exercise:

Try your own piece of timed writing.

Here are some topics.

Spring.
An umbrella.
Lunch.
An orange.
Look out of the window
Rainbow
Sky
Lemon
Jacaranda
Hairbrush
Shower
Riding on a Bus
Crash
Pain
Anger
Sadness

"Writing sooo fast my words are catching fire. I am seeing supercharged poetry!"

188

Using colour to make imagery

A good way to include imagery in poetry is to write using colour. Think about the colour before you start to write

Exercise:

List several images associated with a colour and then decide on narrative and associative possibilities. Consider, as you write, the symbolic associations of the colour chosen: e.g., *red*: anger, passion, *blue*: depression, transcendence, *white*: purity, emptiness, blankness, *black*: anger, darkness, etc.

You may also want to consider the personal associations a colour holds for you.

Here is an example:

1: What things LOOK blue*? lavender, cornflowers, Ulysses butterfly, kingfisher, hummingbird, shark.*

2: What things SOUND blue? *jazz, blues music, poetry, wolf, waterfall.*

3: What things SMELL blue? *Rain, peppermint, incense, cooking, water droplets, freshness.*

4: How does blue FEEL? *cool, soft, relaxing, serene.*

5: What makes YOU FEEL blue? *loneliness, grief, birds singing, watching nature.*

6: What things TASTE blue? *blueberries, wine, peppermints, toasted almonds.*

7: What EXPERIENCES or IDEAS seem blue? *Relaxation, rest, sleep, listening to falling water, pictures water or views of water, grief, depression, sadness, opera.*

8: Can you think of blue PLACES? *Grottos, lakes, the sky, cemetery.*

I expect you will have many different things to add to the list of blue items. Add them. Then do the same with a different colour.

Exercise: Write a poem in which the name of a colour is frequently repeated throughout the course of the poem. If possible, put the name of the colour into the title of the poem. Here are some example:

Blue Note by Samantha Beardon

Have you seen the sky?

in daytime blue or shades of pearly grey

what shade of blue today?

azure clear and sparkling

190

muddy grey or somewhere in between

sky goddess you never stay the same

your companions mirror your mood

the bright orb adding lustre

a jewel flashing bright

changing the spectrum

of your blue face to rosy and fair

Have you seen the sky?

in daytime blue

her transparent snow-white veil's

trailing covering much of her face

on days of sadness she hides her beauty

behind her veils of opaque grey

unwilling to allow mere mortals to

share her pain.

blue blue like the sky a butterfly

the colour of peace spirals upwards

sky goddess hold him safe for me

as your grey veils cover the sun

he is precious.

Sensory Audit.

It is good to go out somewhere with your notebook and do a little surveillance for your poetry, Go sit in a café or in church, or in a shopping mall. I want you to go and look. Listen, touch, taste and smell the environment. Eavesdrop on conversations, the words and the sounds, jot down notes to use in a poem or two or three. This will give you an amazing amount of material for sense-bound writing.

This is a chance to ditch your default impressions and see with new eyes. See the possibilities of the mundane and putting them into poems. Obviously, some subjects lend themselves to one sense more than others but try thinking about and pushing other senses. This is about experimenting with ideas and materials and can be fun, informative and lead you to some interesting poems.

Figurative Language

Figurative (or **non-literal**) **language** uses words in a way that deviates from their conventionally accepted definitions in order to convey a more complicated meaning or heightened effect. Figurative language is often created by presenting words in such a way that they are equated, compared, or associated with normally unrelated meanings.

It is the dressing up of concepts and ideas in interesting ways to engage the reader. There are many literary devices that fall into the category of figurative language; we will look at the most common ones such as simile, metaphor, and some rarer ones, like metonymy. Instead of examining each individual device, let's look at big categories. Some figurative language uses expressions – idioms. Some offer comparisons –

Poetic Comparisons

The most common and important form of figurative language comes when poets compare one thing to another.

Comparison is a literary device in which a writer compares or contrasts two people, places, things, or ideas. This is not a tool just for writers; in life we do it all the time, many times a day. Comparisons allow us to communicate in a vivid pictorial way. Each country will have expressions which get used to express ideas. In England we might say *'She has a heart of gold.'* meaning she is kind. *'It's raining cats and dogs'* meaning it's raining very hard so pictures of what we are expressing rather than a less interesting literal explanation. Hopefully you can see already the poetic value in embracing the use of comparison.

In general, writers use different kinds of comparison to link an unfamiliar or a new idea to common and familiar objects. It helps readers to understand the idea or see a new way of expressing a concept. New concepts can be easier to grasp when viewed with a comparison to something that is familiar.

Using various literary tools for comparison increases the chance of catching the attention and interest of readers, as comparisons help them associate the imagery in a poem to their knowledge of the world.

The major types of comparisons that the new poet should become adept in are, *simile, personification, metaphor.*

194

There are other comparison types all with their own place but poetry, as with other skills means incremental learning.

Simile

A poetic comparison between unlike objects that incorporates the words *'like'* or *'as.'*

Personification

A poetic comparison that gives human qualities to something nonhuman.

Metaphor

The most important comparison, for poetry. A type of analogy that compares two unlike objects with one another. It is one of the biggest ways to set imagery. One we use every day for living. Metaphor flourishes in literature, not just because it is stylistically special, but because it draws freely and often exuberantly on ideas and cultural contexts for its effect.

Symbolism

Symbolism refers to the attribution of ideas and qualities to objects and concepts and abstractions. Symbols represent an idea used in poetry to convey tone and meaning. Like the red rose for love and romance. Symbols can also be categorised as literary or contextual used to go beyond the traditional meaning. They reflect the internal state of mind as revealed through the images. Night represents traditionally grief, death, and in a contextual sense as loneliness, fear or emptiness

Metonymy

A literary device in which is used to describe the whole of a thing related to it. E.g. *The crown for the monarchy.*

Synecdoche

A figure of speech where a part of something describes the whole. E.g. *Fins cut the water.*

In his Rhetoric, Aristotle introduces us to the active metaphor that quickens the readers mind.

He cites the way Homer brings inanimate objects to life giving the example of spears *'standing fast in the ground, while longing to feed on flesh.'* His term 'metaphor' covers a broader spectrum of figurative devices than we might today, although the tools of

196

comparison could all come under the umbrella of symbol or metaphor. The idea is to understand the broad brushstroke idea of the tools when writing a poem, it is creating the image experimenting with words that is important. Have you written a metaphor is it a symbol is it personification? In your early writing don't get hung up on it. What is important is that you have created a vivid picture for your reader. Yet to do that you do need to understand how to utilise the devices so we need to look in some detail how you can produce the imagery to make your words sing.

When is a cup of coffee like a glass of wine? Huh! Never!!

Find the Page

Out of my mind onto the page,
Ideas stream words just rage,
Creativity tantalises, pushes the pace,
The need to transcribe, a daily race,
Clamouring for release urging me on,

My love for life drives the marathon,
Creativity tantalises, pushes the pace,
The need to transcribe, a daily race,
Wanting to engage to evoke a reaction,
Portraying all of life immense satisfaction,

Creativity tantalises, pushes the pace,
The need to transcribe, a daily race,
Writing a need hard to replace
Metaphors similes cut to the chase
Out of my mind onto the page
Happiness sadness bouts of rage
Needing the whole world to engage

Samantha Beardon ©

Simile

A simile describes something by comparing it to something else, using *like* or *as*:

The snake moved like a ripple on a pond.

The object of a simile is to spark an interesting connection in a reader's or listener's mind.

Similes and metaphors are often confused with one another. The main difference between a simile and metaphor is that a simile uses the words *"like"* or *"as"* to draw a comparison and a metaphor simply states the comparison without using *"like"* or *"as"*.

An example of a simile is: *She is as mean as an angry rattlesnake.* An example of a metaphor is: *She is an angry rattlesnake.* Do you see the difference? The simile makes a direct comparison, the metaphor's comparison is implied but not stated.

We use similes a lot in everyday language they help build mind pictures when we talk.

Exercise:

Jot down 6 similes you use regularly.

Similes and idioms tend to be country- or culturally-specific, which can be an issue for people who are reading and writing poetry in a second language.

Similes can make our language more descriptive and enjoyable. Writers, poets, and songwriters often make use of similes to add depth and emphasize what they are trying to convey to the reader or listener. Similes can be funny, serious, mean, or creative.

Explicit similes are those in which the characteristic between the two objects is stated. An **Implicit** simile is one in which the reader must "infer" the specifics of what is being compared. The following simile demonstrates both examples:

Barbara is fast like a greyhound

This is an EXPLICIT simile as it indicates what characteristic of Barbara and the greyhound are shared – specifically, their speed:

200

Barbara is like a greyhound

This is an example of an IMPLICIT simile as the reader need to determine how Barbara is like a greyhound

Does the author mean greyhound like in terms of speed? Or is Mandy perhaps a fast character? Or does the writer mean both? Without further context, it is up to the reader to come to their own conclusion and infer what is IMPLIED with the simile.

Implicit similes contain much more dreaming room and opportunity for the reader to bring their own experience to the poem. Dreaming room will be explored later in this module.

When using similes in poetry overall, it's good to find new and different comparisons to the ones we use in everyday speech. Everyday similes become predictable and overused (cliché) so you need to become innovative in finding new ones if you want your poetry to sing.

The way to find new similes is like finding new and fresh metaphors, I have addressed this later in the book.

It is often possible to make a simile and metaphor from the same root.

anger is like an earthquake - simile

anger is an earthquake - metaphor

work is like a treadmill - simile

work is a treadmill - metaphor

summer is like a hot potato - simile

summer is a hot potato – metaphor

Like the head of a Roman fesco

From **La Giralda** by Samantha Beardon

Before Lake Victoria laps

At your feet like a puppy

Jacaranda Blue on Blue by Laurie

202

Here is a poem, poet unknown, using similes for friends:

Friends are like chocolate cake

You can never have too many.

Chocolate cake is like heaven -

Always amazing you with each taste or feeling.

Chocolate cake is like life with so many different pieces.

Chocolate cake is like happiness, you can never get enough of it.

Exercise:

Find this poem on the internet and see how the poet has handled similes:

"A Lady" by Amy Lowell, who brings the description of a woman to life with similes:

Similes can be either explicit or implicit depending on how the simile has been phrased.

Exercise.

List poems are an interesting genre and you should try writing one in relation to sound. Here is part of a list poem using the senses and using similes.

The ping of the notifications on the mobile phone is
like being stung by nettles

like a pea under ten mattresses

like the laugh of the hyena

like wearing shoes that pinch and cause blisters

like a fire alarm on a desert island

like the tail end of a hurricane

like the echoes of an avalanche

like the sound of chattering teeth from hypothermia

like a road drill outside the bedroom in the middle of the
night

like a fishhook stuck in the finger

like the sound of fighting cats

like the smell of unwashed socks

like biting into a mouldy peach

like the first jolt from the electric chair

like the ringmaster in the circus.

Choose a sound and indulge in an orgy of similes. Have fun!

What Is a Metaphor?

A metaphor is a literary device in which we say one thing is another thing. It is an indirect comparison and we use them all the time in everyday speech. Metaphors aren't meant to be taken literally, they are there to add imagery and context to a scene.

Metaphors often engage our senses by connecting an otherwise abstract subject to sight, sound, smell, touch, taste or motion. If you can engage any of these senses through metaphor, your writing will become vivid, entertaining, memorable; it will be easier for readers to relate to what you're saying, because they can experience it viscerally.

Metaphors also simplify complex concepts, making them easier to understand and digest.

The type of metaphor we use in every day speech are things like:

a step in the right direction

to sell like hot cakes

These tend to be overused. As with the similes, for poetry we need to make metaphors new, fresh and dynamic.

When I say, *"Life is a patchwork quilt,"* you know I'm speaking figuratively. Life is not a patchwork quilt. What I'm saying is that life is made of periods of time, some good and bad, different phases sewn together some holding memories, some frayed and worn but together making a beautiful and unique thing.

A metaphor expresses the unfamiliar tenor in terms of the familiar vehicle. If you call a lively or driven person a "dynamo" *("The guy was a real dynamo.")*, the person is the tenor and *"dynamo"* is the vehicle. A metaphor's comparison is indirectly an implied comparison; It is saying something is something else.

The metaphor can be a comparison of two widely different things, but those things should have at least one characteristic that hooks them together. It is not a case of thinking I want a metaphor for ink so I will pluck any word from my head to make a metaphor.

Ink is a shark perhaps takes a little coming to terms with and will leave your reader puzzled. *Ink is a squid* is too literal as squids produce an ink-like substance.

Ink is the oil that lubricates the engine. Perhaps? You may well find symbolism within metaphors.

There are many different metaphor types. We will just work on the most common.

Types of metaphor

If you Google *types of metaphor* you will get up to 8 different metaphor types and depending on which site you look at you will find different names. I will leave that as a task for you. I want to concentrate on the principle of metaphor rather than engage with every type. I want to highlight:

Direct or simple metaphors

Indirect metaphors

Hidden metaphors

Simple (direct) metaphors

x is y - *grief is a shadow*

the y of x - *the shadow of grief*

x's y - *grief's shadow*

We have direct metaphors such as:

Love is a rose - x is y

The rose of love - y of x

Love's rose - - x's y

My tears a volcano

My volcano of tears

Tear's volcano

Exercise:

Write a set of simple metaphors that run through all three forms:

x is y

The y of x

X's y

Implied Metaphors

While simple metaphors make a direct comparison between two things, saying that one thing is the other, not all metaphors are as easy to understand. Implied metaphors don't directly state both objects being compared. Instead, they describe one with characteristics both have in common, words you would typically use to describe the other.

For example: *The girl hunted her boyfriend before finally pouncing on her prey.*

In this case, the girl is being described as something else, but what is it? The word *hunted* and the phrase

208

pouncing on her prey give a clue. These words are often used to describe predatory animals, such as a tiger or lion. By describing the girl this way, the writer is making an implied comparison that the girl and a predator, without coming out and saying it.

Implied metaphors can be difficult to figure out when you're first learning about them, since you have to trust imagination to understand what the comparison is about. Or be able to do some logical deduction.

A teacher snapped at the child. Comparing the teacher or the teacher's action to a dog or a crocodile.

The simple metaphor the teacher is a dog, wouldn't be very nice and wouldn't necessarily hold a vivid picture. Whereas one can imagine a naughty child and a harassed teacher.

Pat lured James into her web. Pat set out to catch James and she trapped him ...maybe as a lover and she was acting like a spider catching its prey.

Implied metaphors are interesting because they allow vivid imagery.

Some paint a straightforward picture but others make the reader pause to think to make the connection.

She purred over her new coat.

Compares her to a cat.

Implied metaphors often are used to give a double meaning to poems.

What metaphors could you think of for ink?

Let's look at some of the metaphors our poets have used:

Temper Tantrum by Ruby Pond:

I blew my lid when things got tough

Sands by Eric Keizer: *Sands of fate, slowly move*

From **Armistice** by David John Terelinck:

Spilled milk and breadcrumbs,

war crimes of domesticity,
destroy the ceasefire of irritable
silence. Our granite-top DMZ
disappears beneath a salvo
of censure, a strafing attack
on my ability to care for anyone
other than myself.

Scar Tissue by Susannah Bailey:
Which makes my heart quicken
It's scar tissue simply
Beginning to thicken

Sands by Eric Keizer:

The Giza in my soul

Exercise

Use these words to write some metaphors.

Crossbow

Collision

Rainbow

Funeral

Smile

Bend

Crash

Avalanche

Rainbow

Here is a new poem by Laurie Grove told in metaphor. Emotions alluded to by metaphor, the only one named is Love, the counterpoint to the harshness of the images.

A Ghost In The Smoke by Laurie Grove

I have burned with it;
Daubed in sulphur
On a pyre piled high,
Hair sizzling in halo;
Flesh off the bone;

Lungs scoured
In the wind-rush howl,
All voice sucked silent,
Last night's passion;
Reduced to a bed of ash.

The cinders of
A morning wasteland;
Pored over for a trinket;
Some smouldering tissue,
Once tender, now a charred
Husk; no more than
Conflagrated blown dust.

Love? Yes, I know of it.
I hover over its remains;
A ghost in the smoke.

How do we find new innovative metaphors?

Essentially, a metaphor works by revealing some third thing that two ideas share in common. One good way of finding metaphors is by asking these two questions:

What characteristics does my object/idea have?

What else has those characteristics?

Answering the second question usually releases a veritable flood of possible metaphors.

If you look at the word *avalanche,* what characteristics does it have?

Here I have picked a few ideas.

Powerful

Unpredictable

Dangerous

Triggered

Sound

Falling Debris

Silence

Now if I wrote the metaphor

Superman is an avalanche.

      Would you wonder at my sanity?

Until you consider Superman powerful, unpredictable, noisy. Then you have a strong link between the two ideas.

With metaphors there should always be an identifiable link. The poet should never just pull any old idea out of a hat.

I sometimes challenge people when I can't fathom a line or two. Frequently, I am told it's a metaphor, but if it doesn't make sense to the reader then it's a failed metaphor.

If I come up with the metaphor *love is a cabbage*, it probably isn't the best metaphor. I would have my readers puzzled.

Hard, round, green, a dry and tasteless vegetable, unpleasant smell when cooked.

Love is a Mango would be better. Sweet, juicy, tactile, smooth texture. If the relationship between two ideas is not clear, always ask the two questions as they can open up these relationships and help you develop metaphor-seeking habits.

What characteristics does my object/ idea have?

What else has those characteristics?

You come to implied metaphors in a similar way as direct metaphors. You think in the same way, but you modify y to be a characteristic of y.

If you think of the x is y

you start off with the ideas:

motorcycle (x) is a big cat (y)

then you think characteristics of big cat do you replace the cat with them

The motorcycle *crouched* before the race, *growling* in anticipation. (Compares it to a big cat)

The *crouched* and *growling* being characteristics of a big cat.

We can use words to make exciting metaphors through collisions of ideas. You can combine nouns, verbs, adjectives and adverbs to make new metaphors.

Alternatively, you can work from a lexical standpoint you can group according to topic. You can make

215

word sets that can be combined from groups such things as body parts, transport, the weather.

With the body you could list as many body parts as you wanted and turn them into metaphors.

Feet, hands, legs, arms, head. The body is your oyster!

We already have some in body-term metaphors in common use such as:

The foot of the stairs

The heart of the countryside

To give a hand

If you wanted to use these ideas as metaphors in poetry you would have to come up with fresher more interesting metaphors so, get scribbling.

Or you use the brainstorming methods already outlined.

Getting your metaphors right is a huge part of writing vivid evocative poetry. It's important to spend time exploring this use of words and concepts.

Just think:

Even the words *literally* and *figuratively* can be figurative language. Which is the beauty of our chosen medium the amazing elasticity of words! *Figuratively* means metaphorically and *literally* means something that is true. *Literal language* means just what it says whilst *figurative language* uses language away from conventionally accepted meanings add richness and context.

Yet even those words that describe how we use language get used figuratively.

They are going to literally produce a tide of data. - not a tide, just lots!

We literally had fish swimming across the floor. - maybe we did but more likely just water, you can make your own picture.

Protestors literally filled Hong Kong's airport today

The protest was literally like lemmings jumping off a cliff

The music at the rock concert literally blew my head off - exploding heads I don't think so, but you get the idea.

We use figuratively to mean something didn't really happen.

Figuratively speaking they are still in the same boat.

How to rethink those old and clichéd metaphors.

Metaphor use is so common in everyday speech that we will inevitably put them into our poetry because we use certain metaphors so much, they have become clichéd.

Some topics such as love and romance are the subject of millions of poems, so a love poem made up of clichéd phrases becomes rather boring to read, a regurgitation of the theme, something that is not memorable because it's all been said before. Therefore, we need to take the topic and find new ways of expressing it, we need to catch worn-out clichés and replace them with vibrant new metaphors.

Many metaphors we use have become clichéd such as

Her eyes as limpid pools

Her skin white as snow

The moon is a balloon

How can you approach this cliché? Her eyes as limpid pools, meaning her eyes are beautiful.

Brainstorm *eyes* and *beauty* and see what sort of things you come up with that would combine to make interesting metaphors:

218

eyes. for seeing, open, closed, colour...blue, brown, green, grey, flexed.... words to describe their beauty .... stars reflected in a lake.

Other ideas about eyes: epicentre of a storm, half of a closure for clothing, entry to the soul.... mirror, shows expression, beauty of the eyes.

Compare to: the big eyes of antelope, the long-lashed eyes of the giraffe, stars, hummingbird, butterfly, dragonfly, flowers - harebells, violets, bluebells, cornflowers, forget me not. Chestnut, hazel nut, moon, stars, pearls, diamond, sapphire emerald, agate, silver, opal ocean...blue or grey ...sunlight sparkling on it, lakes and pools, wells light, lamps, brightness, clarity, torch, sparkle, glimmer, expression in eye, dreaming, wistful, direct stare, sparkling, depth of colour shifting colour, kaleidoscope, skeins of silk.

From that list you can find loads of new metaphors.

New Metaphors:

Her eyes the colour of polished chestnuts flecked with copper.

Her eyes incomparable emeralds chased with gold and silver.

Her eyes flash with the iridescence of a kingfisher

219

Her eyes are hummingbirds.

Her eyes fire opals changing in the light of candles.

Her eyes soft and dramatic as swans paddling on dark water.

Her eyes blue cornflowers open to the sun.

Her eyes as the soft muted light focused through a Tiffany lamp.

Her eyes are polished chestnuts.

Her eyes are incomparable emeralds.

Her eyes are kingfisher.

Her eyes are fire opals.

Her eyes are swans paddling on dark water.

Her eyes blue cornflowers.

Her eyes are Tiffany lamp.

The ways in which a writer can use metaphors in their poetry are broad and vast. Read as much as possible and study the beautiful words of famous poets with effortless metaphorical prose; Shakespeare, John Donne, John Keats, Maya Angelou and Mary Oliver.

Other Figures of Speech used for Comparison

Personification

Another important Figure of Speech we use for comparison is personification. This occurs when you treat abstractions, animals or inanimate objects as human, that is, giving them human, powers, or feelings nature wept, or the wind whispered to me. The flowers danced in the wind; the rain kissed my skin. These add vividness to expressions, as we always look at the world from a human perspective.

Writers and poets rely on personification to bring inanimate things to life, so that their nature and actions are understood better. It is easier for us to relate to something that is human, or which possesses human traits, its use encourages us to develop a perspective that is new as well as creative. Personification can make a poem engaging create different effects, enhance the poems theme.

Here are some examples from poetry:

Coffee is personified and the lover is also an extended metaphor for coffee.

Tangoing goats and somersaulting hearts
Is that your secret - your charm
you energise goats, mesmerise people

221

your antics boost the weary
wire the unwary yet add clarity to life.

You are my solace, friend, lover
I warm my hands on your hot body
My heart races as my lips trace
The contours under your skin.

Your fragrance distinct pungent
with smoky undertones draws me
My lips are drawn in an erotic
dance my tongue laps at your essence.

My lips are covered in creamy bubbles
As I lift my head reluctantly away
Inhaling your pheromones as I
smile at you with adoration.

My heart skips and somersaults
thuds and thumps, it seems you
can make hearts dance like goats
I want to love you
Stay true to you
but I know
this is our last touch as lovers.

Next time we meet it will
be as acquaintances
I will smell your distinctive
pheromones, remember your
taste your heat I will nod
but regretfully I will
not kiss you.
You are a poisonous drug you scar my heart.

In **Jacaranda: Blue on Blue**

Laurie Grove personifies the Jacaranda tree; it is the narrator.

Every week she passes
Beneath me on her way
From the clinic in Kampala.
She rests awhile in my arms,
And marvels at the sky
Through the veil of my bloom;
Blue on blue.

In Sentimentally speaking the table is the narrator of
the poem.
So, sentimentally speaking, I ask
who am I?
Am I merely a piece of furniture?
Or am I a part of this family?

Exercise:

Write a poem using Personification; either start from scratch or continue these lines:

The piano waits to be played

The dust searches for your fingerprints

The roses search for the sound of your voice

223

Further Reading

Because I couldn't stop for Death by Emily Dickinson.

The Sick Rose by William Blake.

I wandered lonely as a cloud by William Wordsworth

Take a Poem to Lunch by Denise Rodgers.

Symbolism

Symbolism refers to the attribution of ideas and qualities to objects and concepts and abstractions.

The meaning is always very different from the original meaning of the object and from its literal sense.

It can also be the actions of a character, word or action that has deeper meaning in the context of the whole poem.

For example:

The sun as a symbol for light and hope.

The heart and *the red rose* are used as symbols for love.

The dove for peace.

224

Poets use the pen as a symbol for writing poems or ink.

If we want to show at an emotion, we could use symbolism.

Sometimes, an action, an event or a word spoken by someone may have a symbolic value. For instance, *smile* is a symbol of friendship. Similarly, the action of someone smiling at you may stand as a symbol of the feeling of affection which that person has for you.

Symbols do shift their meanings depending on the context they are used in. *A chain*, for example, may stand for union as well as imprisonment. Thus, symbolic meaning of an object or an action is understood by when, where, and how it is used. It also depends on who reads the work and their preconceived ideas about the symbol.

A broken mirror could indicate bad luck or separation.

Colours are often used as symbols: white as pure, blue sad, red for anger.

Exercise:

Make yourself a list of symbols and start to collect their meanings and uses it will be a useful adjunct when you are writing.

To develop symbolism in their work, writers utilise other figures of speech, like metaphors, similes, and allegory, as tools.

Why do Poets Use Symbolism?

It is the job of the poet not to take the usage of symbols lightly. When the poet uses objects to represent people and thoughts, it requires readers to use their own experience and the knowledge that a symbol can have multiple meanings. The use of symbols enhances the reading of a poem. Symbols like the season of Spring or cocoons can represent new life, while falling leaves and the end of the year represent death.

The phrase *"a new dawn"* does not talk just about the actual beginning of a new day but also signifies a new start, a fresh chance to begin and the end of a distressing time.

What is the difference between a symbol and a metaphor?

They're related, but generally a metaphor is used to draw a comparison between two distinct objects, whereas a symbol is used a stand-in for a much more complex, and generally more abstract, idea. In literature, a metaphor would typically be used in a specific instance to compare two objects, but a symbol would be used throughout the work as a major part of the theme.

Examples of symbols used in poetry.

In Shakespeare's *Macbeth,* blood is used to symbolise violence and death.

Edgar Allen Poe uses symbols in *Annabel Lee;* he talks about *a kingdom by the sea.* The *sea* being a symbol for the power of nature. The *kingdom* a symbol for tyranny.

William Blake in *Auguries of Innocence* uses symbolism to portray the world as a grain of sand and heaven as a wildflower. Putting the world in its place in the cosmos and showing the size and beauty of heaven relative to the world.

William Blake also used sunflowers as a symbol for humankind in *Ah Sunflower.*

Further Reading

She sweeps with many colored brooms. Emily Dickinson

Mirror. Sylvia Plath.

The Walrus and the Carpenter. Lewis Carroll. Here multiple things are personified.

Daffodils. William Wordsworth.

Tree at my window. Robert Frost.

Metonymy

Metonymy is a literary device in which one representative term stands in for something else. It's a kind of shorthand for a word or phrase is replaced with another word associated with it. For instance, *"the Crown"* is a metonymy for monarchy rule. A king wears a crown — which is where this metonymy originated — but "the Crown" does not just refer to the king. It refers to the whole system. Similarly, *"the White House"* is a metonymy for the Executive Branch of the United States government.

We use metonymy in everyday speech too if you ask someone to lend a hand, you want help.

The pen is mightier than the sword; we know that a pen isn't stronger than a sword, but we know the pen is being used to refer to the power of words.

How Do You Identify Metonymy?

Metonymy is sometimes confused with two other literary devices, synecdoche and metaphor:

Synecdoche is a figurative term, and is a close relative of metonymy. Synecdoche takes an element of an object and uses it to refer to the whole. If you said *"I see fins swimming across the sea"*, it wouldn't be a disembodied fish, the term would refer to the whole fish. You might refer to your car *as "your wheels"*, that's synecdoche. If you refer to your car as *"your ride"* that would be metonymy. You may use *"bubbly"* to represent champagne. Synecdoche can elevate language making a line feel more poetic. It can also help create a strong voice for a narrator. *"Take thy face hence"*. *Macbeth*, William Shakespeare

Metaphor makes a direct comparison between two things that are not typically thought of in the same way in order to illustrate a clear meaning. *"My life is a train wreck"* is a metaphor.

In the example of metonymy, the Crown is neither a direct comparison nor part of the whole. The best way to think of metonymy is to consider it a "logo" that represents an entire system, which has been distilled down to its essence.

Further Reading.

Out – Out by Robert Frost

Nine to Five by Roger McGough

Allegory

From the ancient Greek to speak or imply.

An allegory is a story, poem or picture that has a hidden meaning often a moral. They can be exciting because they use character and events to show meaning and the meaning is slowly revealed. Allegory uses symbolism, imagery and moral or philosophical, or religious aspects and may include personalisation and abstractions.

Allegories are often written to teach ideas and principles often with a moral dimension.

Although an allegory uses symbols it is different in that it is a complete narrative that involves characters and events that stand for an abstract idea or event.

Allegory is not easily identified in everyday life. Many pieces of literature are allegories such as George Orwell's *Animal Farm*.

The Masque of the Red Death by Edgar Allen Poe is an allegory for death.

Figures of Speech using Expressions and Exaggeration.

Expressions: Idioms

Every language has idioms, which are phrases that cannot be translated literally. The meaning cannot be deduced by the individual words e.g. *over the moon* – meaning to be pleased.

To see the light – to understand. *Bite the bullet* – accept what is going to happen because it's inevitable.

Idioms often originate from metaphors that were once new but people liked so much that they became part of everyday speech. For instance, the idiom *'Set my teeth on edge'* was a metaphor William Shakespeare wrote in *Hamlet.*

Idiom examples:

Get cold feet

Cross your fingers for luck

Sometimes the use of idiom can help you place a poem or the speaker of a poem geographically. Many idioms are clichés though, so use with care.

Exaggeration: Hyperbole.

231

Hyperbole is an exaggeration for effect. They tend to be massive overstatements. In poetry, it emphasizes, evokes strong feelings, and creates strong impressions. As a figure of speech, it is usually not taken literally. It can also be used to create humour.

Examples: *"I could eat a horse"* – I am really hungry. *"He is older than the hills".*

In poetry hyperbole can be used to make a whole poem or in separate lines.

In - *To his coy Mistress* Andrew Marvel used hyperbole to show he treasured her:

*In my poem **on my bed** I used hyperbole.*

As big as two football pitches.

Further Reading:

The Portrait. Stanley Kunitz.

As I walked out one evening. W. H. Auden

Daffodils. William Wordsworth.

Show and Tell

I wish this phrase had not been coined, but it is used widely in literature in both poetry and prose. It's a case of understanding and embracing the concepts seeing past these words. This subject is closely related to using imagery and whether you use concrete or abstract words and phrases. Therefore, some of the concepts will be ones we have already considered, remembering that the poem is the sum of many of our poetic tools.

What do we mean by *show not tell?* When literally every word we use is telling. All words make a progression of ideas. Words give the what, where, who, how of situations. Every poem is made of words strung together into concepts; some poems will have their words stitched smoothly together, others less so.

In the literal sense, telling is putting words on paper or talking.

However, it can also mean giving the bare facts of a situation or using abstract words and expecting the reader to be on the same wave length, telling the reader they are in love, she is beautiful, she is kind. Those words paint a picture there, but it's bald, it's abstract. We are back to the issues we looked at with concreteness and abstraction. The reader must visualise the love, the beauty, the kindness, and they may people your poetry with wonderful images, but their view may be widely off the mark from where you want to take the reader. They might also read those words you have so faithfully crafted and fail to engage; they may skim over them, fail to grasp the meaning and just move on without truly seeing the depth of what you are trying to portray.

What then is *showing*? Showing is adding context to words.

Words sit cosily on the page until along comes the reader.

The reader has different life experiences, expectations and ideas from the poet.

Does that matter? It could. The reader is going to interpret those words the poet has so carefully written into pictures and scenarios. Without context the reader will see the scene from their viewpoint and not tune in to the poet's message.

We do this all the time in our daily lives; we listen, get half the story but we make it a complete story, because we jump to our own conclusions. We fill in the gaps. If you don't add context for your reader, they only have half the story and they may not be hooked to continue reading.

If cause and effect, emotions, sensations are not clear, our brains, which want a total picture, will fill in the gaps to complete the picture for us! So, a poet should enable the reader to see what they are seeing, hearing, feeling, not just tell the stark facts. Readers also want involvement, so giving them a clear picture but allowing enough room for the reader to blend their own pictures with the poetic is what makes for a poem that stands the test of time.

If the narrator of a poem says, *'I am in pain when I look at you'*...really? do I care?

Is it the pain of a grazed knee or a cut finger or a fishhook stuck in my eye or somewhere in between?

'The room is beautiful'....my idea of beauty; a comfy chair, a pile of books. Is this the beauty you mean or is it something more visceral? Does the poet want the reader to see nuances of colours, textures, tones of light and dark? If they are lucky that is what the reader will see. If they are not, their imagery will have by passed the reader by. If it's a metaphor, it's lost.

I often ask poets what lines mean because they make no sense to me and they tell me- "oh that means marriage and that means divorce" or some such explanation. Well, no it doesn't, because they have left me, the reader, with no experience and no context.

Showing is about filling in those gaps for the reader, usually with concrete not abstract imagery.

Show is not about clever word games, using metaphors, puns and similes. It might be, but showing can happen without any of these. The best showing is often that couched in concrete terms. In every good poem we show and tell, you need to train yourself to know when each is the right device to use.

Showing is what fleshes out the heart of a poem, the idea the poet wants the reader to take with them. The vividness and glow of the words.

If the poet tells me they are happy, I can empathise that they are in a good place, but happiness is abstract; you can't touch, taste, smell or hear it. Happiness is not a static state, it changes. For the reader to really be able to understand the message the poet needs to supply some context, then I can visualise what they see, feel, hear. Then I can experience it too.

Life as a poet is about observing carefully and noting every detail. The art of showing begs you to use some of those details in your poetry. Please note I used the word *some*. As with everything there must be balance.

How we move from *telling* to *showing*:

236

As a poet it's about using as many senses as possible. Using those senses will change a poem of telling into one of showing and sharing. When we write we tend to mainly use vision, and within vision we use colour, shape and texture. But we have the other senses; smell, taste, touch, hearing and motion. The more you incorporate senses into your writing the more it will come alive. We are back to the concept of clear imagery.

The senses help with showing instead of telling. It enables the use of concrete imagery rather than abstract imagery to enable the reader to be part of the poem. *Telling* assumes the reader is not smart enough to work out details, that they need information like a lesson. A poem is not a lesson. The reader doesn't need everything explained like the solution to an equation. Poetry and fiction are supposed to mostly excite and entertain. Poetry and fiction work best if they involve the reader... telling the reader that self-sacrifice is best is not as good as showing self-sacrifice in action. It allows the writer to get a deeper message across.

Think: would you rather watch a show on television yourself or have someone tell you about it? Showing allows the reader to be more involved in the emotion of a piece of writing.

If I write *I am sad* - what do you feel? ...sorry maybe??

Do you think 'oh shame the narrator is unhappy'...is it more than a fleeting thought? Do you really care? Probably not!

If you see my sadness, what I am going through, what I am feeling maybe, then you will cry with me. That is what you want the reader to experience.

So instead of: *He has left me I am so sad.* (telling)

"I am leaving" he shouted and stamped out leaving me alone with no money. I shook, my throat so thick and sore I could hardly speak. (showing).

Human beings want to interact with things in life; being passive is boring, so if all your reader has to do is read the words and move on, they will.

If you write in a way that engages them, they become involved in the story. The reader is a problem solver in life so when reading they naturally make conclusions.

The writer's job is to be subtle in how they make the reader work within the piece; make it too difficult and you may lose them. Make it too easy, you lose them. The writing needs to be a balance. Telling is sneaky ....it slips in!

238

How might you recognise you are telling?

Naming emotions - *she was angry, he hated her, she felt guilty*. Using abstractions, *I want freedom, I am disappointed*, are all too vague.

In order to be involved the reader needs to understand the emotions. How do you involve them?

The emotions we feel are nuanced in life; we feel along a continuum, we do not always react the same. By just stating the emotion you only convey the basic idea, you need to bring out the facets, the strength of feeling.

Maybe the narrator is sad but also underneath, bitter and angry. You won't convey that if you just use *sad*.

Telling also happens if you explain motivations using too.

Which of these openings would tug the reader?

The first day of spring

Tom and I

We sail the loch today

Our sail boat new and untried

This sail our longest get away

239

Or:

The cold dawn roused us from heavy sleep

The numbness we were feeling more than the cold

We stumbled on deck to stare at the grey ruffled loch

Aware this was our first sail to the island

Which provides more drama? The first tells us more, but does the explanation create a word picture? Isn't it like setting a stage? We find out a number of things, and in the classic journalistic sense we've provided a good lead: we offer who (Tom and I), when (Spring), where (on the Loch), why (to try a long sail) and how (in a boat bought the year before). But is it drama?

Note what the second selection keys on: the weather (cold), physical state (numbness), mental state (uncertainty). There's a sense of place in here, of course, because none of these other keys would have meaning unless we had an idea where things were happening. There must be a foundation for feelings and emotions to play against, but feelings and emotions are what appeal to the reader and create a bond between writer and reader. The first selection offers no feelings or emotions, only a recitation of facts which provide information. Drama comes when something happens or when something will happen, and when we have drama, we're going to be *showing* instead of *telling*.

When you read a poem that stimulates and provokes your senses, you draw on images from your own experiences. You shape the images from your mind. They involve you, so the poem becomes about you, or at the very least you are riding firmly with the narrator, experiencing what they are, but from your understanding of the world. That's the power of sense-bound writing. It pulls the reader into the poem by using his own experiences as part of the poem's material.

Why do people read poems? To be wowed, entertained, to relate to a story, to learn something new.

Telling doesn't evoke images in the reader's mind. It interprets the information for the reader and robs them of the opportunity to think and discover the poetic world for themselves.

Showing gives the reader enough concrete examples to create a vivid pictorial they read with their own life experiences and interpret the words accordingly.

Poetry is very much about giving 'dreaming room' to the reader.

Whilst *telling* sometimes has a place, we need more *showing* in poetry. Here are some flags that indicate telling.

To spot telling, read every line carefully. Look for places where you find yourself using one of these red flags for telling.

Look for abstract language.

Abstract, vague, language is likely to be telling.

Whilst we as poets use figurative language, we need to avoid the deliberately abstract.

Look at each of your lines. Can you visualize what's happening? Could you film it?

Example:

Telling: *'She looked sad'*. What exactly does *'looked sad'* mean in this context? We're not getting a mental image from this vague description. So, she's sad .... shame; am I emotionally invested? No.

Showing: *'She stared out of the window standing totally still like a graven statue'*.

Look to see if you are making conclusions.

Listing your narrators' actions, suggesting the conclusions your reader will come to is telling. To

242

show, provide them with enough "evidence" so they can come to the conclusions themselves.

Example: *Telling*: *'It was obvious that he was getting angry'.*

Think about how you could show your readers what it was that made it so obvious that he was getting angry.

Showing: *"What did you just say?" Snarling, he stepped right into John's personal space.*

Showing gives us a description of action, body language, facial expressions, and sometimes dialogue so that we can conclude that he's trying to pick a fight without the author outright telling us so.

Making summaries.

If you sum up what happened, you're telling. Sometimes, I come across a poem that reads like a synopsis and that sums up everything that is happening instead of showing it in actual scenes. That's fine if you are writing a synopsis, but not a poem. Readers don't just want to get a general idea of what happened; they want to see specific details.

Example: *Telling*: *'I loved him, but he left'*

If this is a poem with a scene of high emotion in which the narrator finds love and is rejected, readers want to see that suspenseful moment. Saying *I found love and lost it* doesn't create much of an image in the reader's mind.

If you're not sure if you are showing detailed actions or summing them up, try to act out what your characters are doing. If you can't, you're telling.

Example: *Telling: 'The man attacked her. She tried to defend herself'*. What exactly did the man do? Jump? Grab? Punch? Smack? And how exactly did she defend herself? Kick out? Hide? Scream?

Showing*: 'The man leaped, grabbed her arm and swung her round... She threw up her arm to smack his head'*.

Adverbs

If you find yourself using an adverb, you are usually telling. Whenever possible, cut adverbs. Sometimes, the sentence is just fine without. At other times, you might have to rewrite the sentence and replace the weak verb/adverb combination with a stronger verb that makes the adverb unnecessary.

Example: *Telling*: *"Don't lie to me," she shouted angrily.*

Showing: *"Don't lie to me, dammit." She slammed her palm on the table.*

Her word choice and her action show that she's angry, without stating the emotion.

Example: *Telling: 'She walked slowly down the street'.*

Showing: 'She strolled down the street'.

The adverb *(slowly)* tells your readers how Tina walks; the *strolled* shows it.

Adjectives

Like adverbs, adjectives can also be telling, especially if they are abstract adjectives such as *interesting* or *beautiful*.

Example: *Telling: 'I was afraid'.*

Showing: 'My knees felt wobbly as I fled down the stairs'.

Emotion words

When you're naming emotions, you are telling. Look for adjectives such as *surprised* and *angry,* and nouns such as *amazement* and *confusion*. You might even start a list of the emotion words you use most often, to make sure you can catch them during the revisions. Instead of naming emotions, use actions, thoughts, visceral reactions, and body language to show what your characters are feeling.

You can show in this context by using metaphors or similes.

Example: *'Fear clawed at her like a wild animal'.*

Exercise: Take a poem and read it line by line. Can you detect any of the red flags for telling? Can you picture everything described, or are there abstract words, for example? Check the use of adverbs, emotion words, and filters, as described above. Has the poet used past perfect, which can be a red flag for telling readers about things that happened in the past? Highlight all instances of telling that you can find. How many red flags have you found? If you have found some, think about whether their use is justified in the poem if they work. Then consider these issues in relation to your own poems.

Showing and Telling in Action Here is the sort of poem I often see on Facebook and I wrote this as a show and tell exercise!

I lost you

You don't understand

You can't perceive

How I long for you

How I long for your touch

How much I love you

I try my best to show

my love for you

You seem unable to see

How life could be

Life's a mystery

It's been a misery

My love is so great

You don't perceive

The things I do

My love burns for you

My heart needs a soul

to make it whole

My love I save for you

Oh darling look at me

With pools of love.

I look in your eyes but

I don't see my love.

Many people would like this poem, see nothing wrong with it. It is a mediocre poem. I got my friend David to do a critique on it.

Here it is, take a deep breath; he really didn't like it!

'An uninspired and very ordinary poem that gives the reader nothing to hang on to. Anyone can write "My love is so great" or that "My love burns for you". There is no talent in being able to write 'I love you' on a piece of paper. The true art rests in SHOWING how that love materializes.

Why not SHOW the reader the depth of love this narrator has through deed and action? Through vivid and descriptive writing, the narrator can make this

248

poem come alive. At this stage it is a lifeless statement that is no value-add in the genre of poetry. The poet needs to show an act of love or devotion, with metaphor or simile, that paints an image that unmistakably reveals this love.

As this poem stands it is 24 lines of saccharine nothing. It simply says that the person the narrator loves doesn't recognize this devotion. So what? This could have been said in 2 lines and saved the reader the time and agony of 22 redundant lines. And the overly sentimental cliché is a real turn-off: "pools of love". Eyes as pools for reflection of love has been done to death over the centuries and has no place in modern poetry unless the poem is excellent (which this is not) and another choice of imagery cannot be found (which is highly unlikely). The same goes for burning hearts and empty souls.

This comes off as lazy writing that is mawkish, clichéd and a badly written whinge. The end rhyme is also trite given the lack of substance in the poem. This poem has nothing important to offer the reader about unreciprocated love; nothing that they haven't heard a thousand times before, and via far better poetic expression.'

What can you learn from this?

:

Here is a poem, showing more than telling, peopled with description

You

I look at the video

There is no mistaking you,

Poised by the jeep, surrounded by light

as the sun bounces off metal and glass,

the bright blue sky like a distorting mirror.

Your head thrown back, making a sound, I cannot hear,

Although I am imagining, the infectious

booming roar, rolling from your lips.

I feel you shift, showing

the distinctive muzzle, under the bushy mane,

The dark blue jumpsuit accentuates

the sculpted solidity of your form,

I want to walk towards you, to feel the magnetism

You could turn, and I would be caught

250

mesmerised. By the brightness of your gaze,

Those eyes flecked with gold

dominate your tanned face,

Forever drawing me towards your world.

I see the colours, the colours of the African day,

Reflected in the honey toned clarity of your skin,

The vividness of your eyes, the silver of the

stubble glinting on your chin, the crow's feet

wrinkles, mirroring the drought parched land.

Etched in my memory.

Firm lips. Corners kinked into the hint of a smile,

Open, to speak words in accent less English,

Always a surprise given your antecedents,

There is a hint of croaky graveliness in your diction,

Like the cry of the Eagle

The harshness evident, registering impatience,

251

A man honed by the rituals, hunts and rhythms

of the animal kingdom.

You turn back, then lope lithe as a big cat,

Your controlled movements, denote a man of action,

Sexuality oozes, even from your retreating form,

How can you be defined?

Your charm, friends, words, the books you read, the inner man?

My picture of you has empty squares.

There is a cold breeze raising goose bumps on my skin,

As you disappear into the heat haze,

Hopes, dreams, and beliefs unshared,

Images blown like paper.

Stirring, in the draught from an open window

Whirling, swirling always mine.

Better imagery?

An example of Show and Tell:

Finding the Light   ©Samantha Beardon

I don't think I ever

understood the fundamentals of love

I knew how to care - to be a giver

I wanted to be a receiver

I needed to see love emblazoned across the sky

The dark velvet night covered in a golden

Scatter of stars with the streak of a comet arcing high

Romantic love as displayed by books, poetry and films

I searched for perfect love and I searched

Highs and lows romance and disappointment

In the end I settled for less -

friendship and companionship

Resigned to a lack of fireworks slightly resentful

The dark night sky vast and empty

full of echoing silences

What did I miss?

I don't think I ever

understood that love comes in many guises

Those small thoughtful gestures

Just being there - a rock steadfast in troubles

A listening ear even when

The subject is incomprehensible

Tolerance of habits and foibles

Appreciation and thanks

Sharing the good and the bad

The dark sky filled with stars

like pale corn into freshly turned ground.

Steadfastness

I wanted to see fantasy transient ephemera

When I needed solid dependable caring

The feeling of warmth springing from cold

A promise of life in the darkness

Now I can see you - feel you

Understand what I so nearly threw away

I don't think I understood

  The fundamentals of love

        Until now

The velvet of the night sky alive

with the fluidity of sparkling light

azure, magenta

        and pure gold.

Here you have a mixture of show and tell; you should be able to identify the 'tell' and the use of some 'imagery'. The balance is skewed towards *tell* but feedback on this poem is that the poem works. The mixture of each poem will vary it is finding and thinking about how your poem is working that is the key.

It's all about Prosody!

As a poet you are constantly making choices about meaning, rhythm and sound. We are looking at these elements to help you train your ear, eye and mind, to be alert for the reasons to choose one word instead of another. Not just using gut feeling and base instinct. These ideas and exercises are designed to train your ear, remind you that the first chosen word is not necessarily the best. Those words that came to you in a dream are not inviolable but the start of a process.

If we use music as an analogy in voice leading musical notes transition in a smooth harmonious way This is the effect, you are using in assonance it connects ideas using vowel sounds. When you use assonance at the end of phrases it affects the lyrical structure of your poem making it a definite alternative rhyming technique. If you are using it inside a phrase, then it is about connection between words and leading the sounds forward thus the reader forward so choosing the right word and sonic connection is important. Alliteration is also about sonic repetition and voice leading.

Composers use this technique all the time with music. Poets can do it with the musical sounds and repetitions in poetry. One of the ways to tune your ear is to make worksheets of words and find rhymes, perfect, assonance, consonance, also group the alliterative words together until this becomes so natural it flows in your writing.

256

Prosody

Prosody is the study of all the elements of language that contribute toward acoustic and rhythmic effects, chiefly in poetry but also in prose. The term derived from an ancient Greek word that originally meant a song accompanied by music, or the tone or accent given to an individual syllable.

To write great poetry as opposed to 'ok' poetry one needs to understand how to manipulate language, how words and syllables create sound and how to work with these - the rhythmic quality of speech and of life.

By manipulation of language I do not mean going through a thesaurus and plucking out the most obscure words and using them but being aware of how words work together and how sounds work together to choose the right combination to get the right effects. All the things we have been considering until now.

Don't get hung up on the obscure words related to prosody; all the Latin terms related to poetry theory. Look beyond them to the concepts that will enable you to up your poetic game.

Remember that to master most things you need to understand the fundamentals. Football, painting, driving, swimming; each one has a set of skills attached and poetry is no different.

Those elements of language we need to use get grouped group under the umbrella of a term called **PROSODY**.

Prosodic features are features that appear when we put sounds together in connected speech, they are intonation, stress, and rhythm. This coupled with word choice are the backbone of poetry.

Prosody can be divided in the same way as metre into four main categories:

Syllabic prosody. Accentual prosody

Accentual Syllabic prosody Quantitative prosody

The functions of prosody in poetry are:

> *Syntactical phrasing*
>
> *Word segmentation*
>
> *Accents and Stress*
>
> *Rhythm*
>
> *Underscoring emotion.*

Because prosody relates to intonation, stress and rhythm it sets the tone of speech and concepts. It will be responsible for highlighting not only the speed of delivery but the emotions. Prosodic features will highlight mood, emotion. It will echo irony, sarcasm, sadness, joy.

Metre is a part of prosody; it is a concept that depends on our knowledge of the stresses of speech. Once poets have mastered the concepts then there are many ways to vary and use rhythm and intonation to create sonic and emotional effects in poetry.

Your stress instead of word stress.

Let's take a moment to stop and think you the poet centre you back in the here and now away from the intricacies of poetic theory. Most of the lessons we need for poetry are also centred around lessons for life. Learn the tools of the trade but let the wisdom of your approach to life aid your ability to write well. One of the things we need to be in life is open to new ideas and new ways of doing things and when things don't work, we need to let go. This applies to the poem we thought was the best we had ever written that others felt needed to work. Let go of the hurt, the indignation and think logically about the comments.

Breathe deep and let your shoulders relax.

You can't get the rhyme right the metre eludes you, put it away, let it go for now later your eyes will be clearer. As you breathe deeply gather up your stress and toss it to the sea and see it carried away. Centre yourself you are ready to begin again poet,

Syllables and word stress

The purpose of language is to communicate as efficiently as possible. Speech is fast; we don't pause between words. As we talk, we shorten some words and glide over some parts of words together.

Each English word is given its own weight or push as we speak it within a sentence. But when we string words together as we speak, we give some words or parts of words stress and some we glide over and some we blend together. Listen. Really tune in to people talking. We talk in a steady stream our languages have ways to allow communication to be efficient. Each language has a way of helping us differentiate syllables and know when to join them together into words.

In English our syllables are said in different keys so they make melody. This enables us to identify multisyllable words; for instance, *allow* has two syllables. When you learn the word, you learn the sounds and a little tune - di DUM - you add pitch (stress) to *low* so it is said *alLOW*. Say the word several times, fast and slow feel the melodic leap on the second syllable.

261

Let's look at these sentences: Say them aloud.

From TIME to TIME and for EVER MORE.

As LONG as the WORLD KEEPS TURNING.

The words that we stress are written in capitals.

We glide over the particles *('from', 'to', 'and', 'for', 'as',)* and give a little push to the important *words ('time', 'ever', 'more', 'long', 'world', 'keeps', 'turning')*. These are the ideas we hear and register.

Also, we tend to accent the operative part of monosyllabic words when extended, so in words like *MOPing* and *QUICKly* we hardly express the *-ing* and *-ly*

As poets we need an awareness of such nuances! Start to tune into the key as well as the sounds, especially of words of more than one syllable.

When we talk, we normally give weight to vowels and their accompanying consonants.

262

A syllable is: *a unit of pronunciation having one vowel sound, with or without surrounding consonants, forming the whole or a part of a word.*

A word can have 1, 2, 3, 4, or even more syllables.

- 1 syllable words: *hi, fun, kites*

- 2 syllable words: *hello, runner, party*

- 3 syllable words: *elephant, fantastic*

- 4 syllable words: *alligator, photography*

Some words, *bone* for example, contain only one syllable (emphasized sound). Other words, such as *hello* (hel/lo) contain two syllables. We have words built from any number of syllables: *Abdominal* has four syllables (ab/DOM/i/nal).

Every syllable must contain at least ONE vowel, as it is the opening and closing of the mouth to say the vowel sound that makes a syllable.

However, it is the NUMBER of VOWEL SOUNDS that determines THE NUMBER OF SYLLABLES IN A WORD, NOT THE NUMBER OF VOWELS.

Words like *bike* and *cake* have two vowels but only one vowel sound. And words like *sound* and *boil* are spelled with vowel teams that make a single vowel sound. As such, these words all have just one syllable. Also note that '*y*' can make a vowel sound as in the words *try* and *fly*.

When we speak in English, we don't just say syllables in a monotone voice, unless we are trying to do a bad impersonation of a robot. Instead, we vary the pitch, volume, and strength of our pronunciation, or stress the syllables; sometimes our meaning may be completely different, depending on where we place that emphasis as we talk.

Syllables are based on vowel sounds and we move our jaw most when we are saying vowel sounds, if you put your hand under your chin when saying a word, you can tell the number of syllables by the movement of your jaw.

Try saying:

main - one syllable

delete -two syllables

constitutional - five syllables.

Practice the technique. It's a good way to identify syllables if the classical form sets the number of syllables per line.

When counting syllables, you count more than single words – you count the entire interconnected phrase, as you would pronounce it, not as it is spelled.

He throws the glass and makes an awful crash

He/ throws/the /glass/and/ makes/an /aw/ful /crash

So, 9 words but 10 syllables.

As we speak, we stress words emphasising the vowel sounds in the words we need people to connect with.

So, nouns, adjectives, adverbs and verbs tend to have stress; they do the work. Particles, prepositions, pronouns and conjunctions are designed to show how the important words relate to each other and they set the lower key to enable important words to be picked out of conversation.

This is useful to remember if you are having to write in metre where you need to balance not only the number of syllables but stressed and unstressed syllables.

In speech there is only one major stress in a word but in a multi-syllable word there is likely to be a secondary stress. In poetry we might utilise that stress in our syllable count. The primary stress will always be higher and louder, but the secondary stress will be louder and higher in pitch than an unstressed syllable.

When we stress syllables in words, we use a combination of different features. Experiment with the word *attractive*. Say it out loud. Listen to yourself. The second syllable of the three is stressed.

atTRACtive

What are you doing so that the listener can hear that stress?

• A stressed syllable combines five features:

• It is l-o-n-g-e-r – *at TR-AC -tive*

• It is LOUDER - *at**TRAC**tive*

• It has a change in pitch from the syllables coming before and afterwards. The pitch of a stressed syllable is usually higher.

• It is said more clearly -The vowel sound is purer. Compare the first and last vowel sounds with the stressed sound.

266

• It uses larger facial movements - Look in the mirror when you say the word. Look at your jaw and lips.

You need to understand syllables in order to understand metre.

Therefore, you must start to be able to identify syllables as the first step.

TIP: To identify syllables in words:

Put your hand under your chin as you say the word you feel your chin drop as your mouth makes a syllable.

Each TIME we TALK we STRING toGETHer STRESSED and THEN unSTRESSED in PATterns NEVer THINKing HARD.

You need to practice breaking words into syllables to understand how rhythm in poetry works.

Exercise:

Find the syllables in the following words.

Wonderful

Sand

Dinner

Calendar

Porcupine

Sneeze

Fire   Answers p.364

Here are a few examples of the various words that might be **unstressed as we talk.** Of course, as with all of grammar there are exceptions to the 'rules.'

Pronouns - *I, we, you* (singular and plural*). He, she, it, they, me, us, her, him, them, mine, your, myself, yourself*

Conjunctions - *and, but, if, because, your, while, where*

Articles - *a, an*

Prepositions - *In, off, an, over*

Auxiliaries - *can, could, be*

The best way to read poetry is aloud.

The choice of words, the number of syllables, and the arrangement in lines will dictate the rhythm; using stressed and unstressed syllables is important to getting a good beat in our poetry.

The time taken to say the word will depend on the number of syllables and where the stress lies. Punctuation will also affect rhythm. Line stops or the running of two lines into the other (enjambment) and in speech the normal pause for a breath will change the way we read the lines.

We always use natural stress but learning and accent sometimes change where the stresses go.

With writing one needs to stick to where the natural stresses are in words unless writing a poem in dialect. Obviously American and British readers will have different syllable accents on some words and regional variations can change things yet again.

Where is the natural stress for you in the following words?

DeCREASE, DEcrease,

CONTroversy, conTROVersy

GARage, garAGE

Sometimes the stress will change according to the meaning or nature of the word.

Sometimes *CIRCumstances* will change *CIRcumSTANCES*

Here are the basic rules that govern stress on words. Note as always there are exceptions!

I have the following laminated on my desk, so I have an aide memoire:

270

Word Stress Rules

There are some very simple rules about word stress:

1. One word has only one stress. One word cannot have two stresses. If you hear two stresses, you hear two words. Two stresses cannot be one word. It is true that there can be a "secondary" stress in some words. But a secondary stress is much smaller than the main (primary) stress and is only used in long words. In classical forms we would often count the secondary stress.

2. We can only stress vowels, not consonants.

3. Information words tend to be stressed; nouns, verbs, adjectives and adverbs. Grammatical words such as prepositions, articles and auxiliaries are mostly not stressed.

4. Bear in mind these are general rules and if course there are exceptions. Nothing is ever simple! But these ideas will help you write better poetry.

The stress on first syllable:

Most 2-syllable **nouns:** *PRESent, PERfume, SPANner, TAble*

Most 2-syllable **adjectives** *PRESent, GENTle, NARrow, HAPpy*

Stress on last syllable:

Most 2-syllable **verbs:** *preSENT, adMIRE, deCIDE, adMIT*

There are many two-syllable words in English whose meaning and class change with a change in stress.

The word *present*, for example is a two-syllable word. If we stress the first syllable, *PRESent*, it is a noun (gift) or an adjective (opposite of absent).

But if we stress the second syllable, *present*, it becomes a verb (to offer).

More examples: the words *export, import, contract* and *object* can all be nouns or verbs depending on whether the stress is on the first or second syllable.

Stress on penultimate syllable (penultimate = second from end)

Words ending in **-ic-** *GRAPHic, geoGRAPHic, impressionIStic*

272

Words ending in **-sion** and **-tion** - *reveLAtion , divISion*

For a few words, native English speakers don't always agree on where to put the stress.

For example, some people say *teleVIsion* and others say *TELevision*. Another example is: *CONtroversy* and *conTROversy*.

American English and British English often have different stress.

Stress on ante-penultimate syllable (ante-penultimate = third from end)

Words ending in **-cy, -ty, -phy and -gy** - *deMOcracy, dependaBIlity, phoTOgraphy, geOLogy*

Words ending in **-al** - *CRItical, geological*

Compound words (words with two parts)

For compound **nouns**, the stress is on the **first part**

SUNrise, BOYfriend,

For compound adjectives, the stress is on the second part

part-TIME, open-MINDed, green EYED

For compound **verbs**, the stress is on the **second part**

underSTAND, overFLOW

A quick resume:

Stress the first syllable of:

Most two-syllable nouns

Most two-syllable adjectives

Stress the last syllable of:

Most two-syllable verbs

Stress the second-to-last syllable of:

Words that end in *-ic*

Words ending in *-sion* and *-tion*

Stress the third-from-last syllable of:

Words that end in *-cy, -ty, -phy* and *-gy*

Words that end in *-al*

Information words are those that are normally stressed. When in doubt try saying the word aloud, try the hand under the chin. Use dictionaries or syllable websites to double check. There are so many resources you don't need to guess.

274

Finding the Stresses in a Poem

Reading a line and listening is a great way to gauge stresses, along with your knowledge of which words are likely to be stressed.

The rhythm of the words in a poem is like the beat in music. This rhythm makes the poem sound musical and interesting to the reader or listener.

Rhythm in poetry is made up of stressed and unstressed syllables or words. The marking of stressed and unstressed syllables is called **Scansion** and is rather akin to marking up a piece of music. In books you will often see unstressed marked with (˘) and stressed syllables marked with (´). These are the symbols you also find in dictionaries. I find these difficult to work with, so I mark a stressed syllable or word in a poem with a (/).

An unstressed syllable or word is shown with an (x).

Or for ease of learning you can just indicate the stressed syllable with CAPITALS.

275

When you are doing scansion, use the system that works best for you. Just be consistent.

To find your stresses in a line, say it out loud several times. Our natural speech pattern tends to be unstressed and stressed syllables alternating although meaning and emotion can change that. Say those words naturally to try to feel the rise and fall.

We do a scansion to identify stressed and unstressed syllables.

For example:

/ x / x / x /

This would indicate stressed unstressed stressed unstressed stressed unstressed stressed syllables in a line.

For ease I often put my stresses into capitals and leave the unstressed syllables in lower case. You will need to work out what works best for you.

It doesn't matter exactly where you put the scansion marks. Somewhere in the middle of the syllable is good, it's hard to get it over the vowel itself but as long as the correct syllable is marked, that is fine.

Examples:

/   x   /   x   /   x   /

PETE and PAT went DOWN the ROAD

/   x   /   x   /   x   /

TWINkle, TWINkle LITtle STAR

/ x   x   x   /   x   x

ALec and I SOMersault

You should hear the cadence as you read, particularly if you read aloud.

Exercise:

Your challenge is to divide this poem into stressed and unstressed syllables:

Mirage shimmering in the heated air

no oasis projected on the desert

just shimmering air

I cannot touch

an abstraction

I do not understand

Mirage shimmering in the heated air

no oasis projected on the desert

just shimmering air

I cannot touch

an abstraction.   Answers p.365

Prosody, Rhythm and Metre

Metre UK, *Meter* American English.

Metre (Measure) is the heartbeat of a classical poem; it is organised rhythm.

Metre comes from the way we use syllables. In normal speech, stresses come at regular intervals – regardless of the number of unstressed syllables in between them. Since our normal language has rhythm the difference between poetry and normal language is not that one is rhythmical and the other is not. It is that poetry shapes the natural rhythms of speech through metre, line length and word choice. In poetry words are arranged in patterns therefore increasing rhythm.

Metre mimics and heightens the rhythm of speech; it comes from within words and is a very powerful tool. Metre is the musical element that involves the stresses of words and the arrangement of those words to create patterns.

Metre works in the same way that musical composition works. Music is the organisation of sounds - Metre is the organisation of soft and loud sounds (or unstressed and stressed syllables).

Classical poetry is built using emphasised syllables in patterns, which allow the words to flow in almost melodic cadence.

However, as I have said before, it is the NUMBER of VOWEL SOUNDS that determines the number of syllables in a word, NOT THE NUMBER OF VOWELS.

Note that Free verse is not metrical. Its lines are rhythmical, we can hear and feel a rhythm. The natural rhythms of speech are shaped by the poet, but not into regular metric patterns. Poets use all the devices outlined in previous chapters to enable flow and cadence in Free Verse.

Metre can be categorised in four ways but generally in English we use *syllabic* and *accentual* metre more, but some forms do require *accentual-syllabic* metre.

Syllabic: The counting of syllables per line

Accentual: A counting of accents (stresses) per line

Accentual syllabic: The counting of syllables and accents (stresses)

Quantitative: Measures the duration of words – not used in English poetry.

As we have already discussed we utilise stressed and unstressed syllables to make the rhythm of speech. In metre, groups of syllables work together to make patterns of sound. Each group of syllables is called a **foot** (because the feet walk along the line).

Syllabic Metre

Many classical forms will give you a syllable count per line and so when you write you need to count the syllables.

I am marking each syllable with /

In/di/vid/u/als/ who/ have/ this /an/im/al /to/tem, - we have 13 syllables.

are/ high/ly/ in/tu/i/tive/ and /ar/ti/sti/cal/ly in/clined. -we have 15 syllables

Exercise:

Here are some for you to practice with:

Today is not a holiday

Tomorrow is another day

Look into my eyes

Syllable counting is easy.

Many classical forms specify the number of syllables per line, and this is how you work out your syllable count.

Examples of syllable counting:

Here are the instructions for a poetry forms--an old Welsh form called the **ENGLYN PENFYR.** It is syllabic and rhymed in nature, as opposed to counting stresses, but the use of internal crossover rhymes lends it a very rhythmic quality.

The poem is comprised of three-line stanzas, and each line has seven syllables and a rhyming word in the seventh position. A three-syllable caesura is added to line 1, which cross-rhymes with the first three syllables of line 2.

Here is the first stanza of **Castle Magic**:

I conjure it with magic- castle fair

Just don't stare, fall or panic

My creation huge gigantic.

I/ con/jure /it /with/ mag/ic- cast/le/ fair

Just /don't /stare, /fall/ or /pan/ic

My/ cre/a/tion /huge /gi/gan/tic.

Count the syllables.

If you count carefully you will find 8 syllables in line 3. Whoops! Now I need to adjust the line to make 7 syllables. I need to replace gigantic which also isn't a perfect rhyme with a two-syllable word that also rhymes with magic.

I/ con/jure /it /with/ mag/ic- cast/le/ fair

Just /don't /stare, /fall/ or /pan/ic

My/ cre/a/tion /huge /trag/ic

Replacing *gigantic* with *tragic* gives us 7 syllables, keeps the rhyme and doesn't really alter the sense of the poem.

Here is another form, the *Terza Rima.* It is written in three-line stanzas with a fixed rhyme scheme and normally written in 10 syllable lines.:

A creator, destroyer, transformer

Which will you be, as you play your guitar?

I wanted love to be your reformer.

A/cre/at/or/de/stroy/er/trans/form/er

Which/will/you/be/as/you/play/your/gui/tar?

I /want/ed/love/to/be/your/re/form/er.

Accentual metre

Accentual metre creates the 'drumbeat' which keeps a poem in perfect time. To keep that perfect time, the poems need to have the same meter, or the same number of syllables in each line, or set of lines.

In accentual metre, syllables are combined into either pairs or trios to create the rhythm and are a mix of stressed and unstressed syllables. These combinations are called **feet**. Think of *metre* as a set of dances; the waltz or the tango, each has a specific set of movements the dancers have to perform with two feet. In metre you create dance moves with combinations of syllables using two types of syllables to move across the line although some of the dancers are alien and tango with three feet.

Iambic metre

The most common metre and the one we use most in speech is a foot called an **iamb,** a pair of syllables working together. It is a rising rhythm.

An unstressed syllable followed by a stressed syllable. As a sound it could be represented as

di DUM

Here are some examples of iambs with the stressed syllable in capitals:

the NIGHT

  di   Dum

each NIGHT

  di   Dum

Pre/SENT

di Dum

As LONG

di   Dum

Ad/JUST

di Dum

An unstressed plus a stressed syllable = iamb

Repeat

The sea

My wife

Distort

The scent

Iambs or other metres are usually repeated across lines and give the strong rhythm in some poetry.

The most typical meter used in English poetry is ten beats or syllables per line divided into 5 pairs (feet) and arranged in unstressed and stressed syllables.

di DUM di DUM di DUM di DUM di DUM

Five sounds repeating like a heartbeat:

and ONE and TWO and THREE and FOUR and FIVE

This 10-syllable, 5-sound rhythm is often used in classical verse in things such as Sonnets.

If you had, for instance, a line made up of this soft/hard syllable combination and there were five pairs. The line would be called a line of pentameter, because there are 5 pairs of poetic feet.

Basically a 10-syllable line, but specifically written in iambic pairs.

Let us see **iambic pentameter** at work in a poem:

The com/posi/tion sets/ a vi/tal spark

The art/ist's hand /unseen, / forev/er hid

286

This study/ a blaze/ is shad/ ed red/ to dark

With waves/ of pass/ion - art/ist's eye/ undid

Here, I marked the feet the iamb pairs with a /.

Note, you are breaking each word into stressed or unstressed syllables, so to find the iambs and make the pairs words get divided and the whole line works together to produce the iambic feet.

Go back and read the stanza aloud and feel the cadence.

This is what you have to achieve when you write a Classical form in iambic pentameter.

Exercise:

Try breaking this stanza down into iambs:

The need to paint compulsion getting strong

His vision blurs his world begins to shrink

The painter deaf to breeze and natures song

His mood I guess as dark as blackest ink

Further reading: poetry in Iambs:

Any Shakespeare Sonnet

Tithonus. Alfred, Lord Tennyson.

Lyrics of *'You gotta help me I'm losing my mind.'*
One Direction.

Now we have looked at the most common metre –
Iambic Pentameter, we now need to look at other
metres.

Iambic (the type of foot) *Pentameter* (the number of
feet on the line – i.e. 5).

Of course, not every poem has lines made up of 5
feet per line it would make life simpler, but it would
make poems all sound similar. Lines of feet come in
various lengths and each has its own name.

Number of Feet: per line:

1 foot: *monometer*

2 feet: *dimeter*

3 feet: *trimeter*

4 feet: *tetrameter*

5 feet: *pentameter*

6 feet: *hexameter*

7 feet: *heptameter*

8 feet: *octameter*

Therefore, you will see poems written in **iambic tetrameter:**

4 feet and 8 syllables per line:

di Dum di Dum di Dum di Dum

or **iambic trimeter:**

3 feet, 6 syllables*:*   *di Dum di Dum di Dum*

Below are two lines in **iambic trimeter**

The end/ must come/ at last

Our fears/ we can't/ allay

You. by Samantha Beardon.

Written in Iambic tetrameter.

I like /your style

You make/ me smile

Your ease/ and charm

Act like/ a balm

The you, /I share

Without /a care

The bits/ I see

Tantal/ise me

Whilst iambic pentameter is a popular form of poetry metre, we also encounter much tetrameter - 4 stresses or beats per line.

Nursery Rhymes, hymns, ballads and many pop songs have the *di dum* structure.

For example, *'Lucy in the Sky with Diamonds'* 1967 by the Beatles.

Other metre forms

There are several different forms of metre, some working on pairs of syllables and some on trios of syllables. Much of this would need to be studied from a more in-depth perspective than can be achieved in this book. I will give you as a starting point the basics.

Here is a list of the different metres and categorised by syllable count, Foot name, sound pattern:

2 syllables: **pyrrhus:**   *di – di*

2 syllables: **iamb:**   *di – DUM* *

2 syllables: **trochee:**   *DUM – di* *

2 syllables: **spondee:**   *DUM – DUM* *

3 syllables: **tribrach:**   *di – di – di*

3 syllables: **dactyl:**   *DUM – di – di* *

3 syllables: **amphibrach:**   *di – DUM – di* *

3 syllables: **anapest:**   *di – di – DUM* *

3 syllables: **bacchius:**   *di – DUM – DUM*

3 syllables: **antibacchius:**   *DUM – DUM – di*

3 syllables: **cretic:**   *DUM – di – DUM*

3 syllables: **molossus:**   *DUM – DUM – DUM*

A huge list, but don't despair. You will commonly see *iambs, trochees, anapests, amphibrachs,* and *dactyls* used. The most important are shown by *.

Metred poems are mostly written in iambs with anapests, trochees and dactyls making appearances.

You learnt how to do a *scansion* earlier on in the book and so you should be able to work out metre from your scansion and the above list.

Trochee

In the trochaic metre you are using your stressed and unstressed syllables in a direct reversal of how they were used as iambs. You place a stressed syllable followed by an unstressed syllable in pairs across the line. *DUM di DUM di.* It is said to be a falling rhythm. It is rare to have a whole poem in this metre but it is used in lines and phrases to give emphasis and to change the rhythm.

Trochee examples:

POetry

TROchee

GARden

HIGHway

TROUble

JUST to LIVE in YOUR time

Here is part of a poem by Miriam Ruff in a form called *The Ravenelle.*

When was life yet filled with brightness, when were things all tinged with rightness,

In the distant past I flourished, happy times were still at hand—

Then came thoughts all filled with sorrow, never gone from day tomorrow.

This is a trochaic form.

293

When would you use trochaic metre?

Trochaic metre because of its falling nature can be plaintive, mournful even. It also moves forward quickly with the rise and fall cadence.

Examples of poems in Trochaic metre:

The Raven by Edgar Allen Poe.

The Song of Hiawatha by Henry Wadsworth Longfellow.

Macbeth by William Shakespeare. (Check out those spells! Hubble Bubble).

Sorrow. By Edna St. Vincent Millay

Trochee, pokee, hokey cokey?

294

Anapest

The anapest is a metrical foot composed of two unstressed syllables and a stressed syllable:

di di DUM di di DUM di di DUM.

Anapaestic metre is rolling and is often used in lighter subjects or in poetry with humour such as limericks.

Examples of Anapests:

underSTAND

underFOOT

overCOME

Many idioms are anapaestic:

Get a LIFE

At the DROP of a HAT

When would poets use anapests? The anapest emphasises the stressed syllable with the two soft sounds between each stress. It gives a sing song like

295

quality that lends itself to children's poetry, comic material. In *The Destruction of Sennacherib*, the poem is about horses and this metre has the feel of galloping horses.

Poems using all anapaests are less common than poems with anapaests as part of mixed metre lines.

Look up *Sea Fever* by John Masefield. Here, anapaests are used with iambs.

Further Reading: Poetry with Anapaests.

The Destruction of Sennacherib by Lord Byron.

There was an old man with a beard. Edward Lear.

A visit from St. Nicholas by Clement Clark Moore.

Using Metre.

Formal forms of poetry take much work and planning. You must work out the line structure of stresses, then think about your words carefully. Once you have the stresses you have the rhythm, but the even cadence can become tedious if the diction is forced to fit the line.

Metre is beautiful if the sounds, meaning and diction all intermesh. When, as we all do, we first write using iambs, trochees or anapests we put the structure first. Sense and diction come second. Meaning yes, it is there but form takes presidency. The classical form is like a puzzle it is hard to write spontaneously out of the head! It must be worked at.

Why bother to learn to write in metre?

Even if you are going to write predominately in free verse the skills in sounds and rhythm you get from learning the discipline of writing in form are invaluable. The skills of planning and editing also become well used. All skills you need for any poetry that you write.

An example of metre, and word choice.

Sometimes syllable counts are less of an issue than the mixing of poetic feet within some of the lines.

As an example, here are 12 syllables, but the line is built of two amphibrachs, followed by two anapests:

the - WIND - feels / eu - PHOR - ic / as - it - GRA / zes - my - FACE

When I try to set it to a beat in my head, it is always easier to do it with catalexis (missing the last syllable) than it is to change beat patterns in the middle. In this, I would change the "as it grazes" anapest to an amphibrach, like "while grazing", then just leave the line catalectic at 11 syllables ... the whole line will then flow.

the - WIND - feels / eu - PHOR - ic / whilst GRA / zing - my – FACE

Feel the difference in the flow?

Exercise: Iambic pentameter lines?

Where green maize fills the fields without sorrow.

Ten boats all jostled hard to gauge the line.

Like ghosts they echo every step I take.

In autumns breeze my world began to turn.

Answers p. 367

298

Rhyme

Our first introduction to rhyme is often in nursery rhymes; playground games, simple songs. Children, when first asked to write poetry nearly always think that they must produce rhymes.

This is a belief which sometimes lingers into adulthood, with the result that there are those, even today, who think that a poem is not a poem unless it rhymes (this includes my husband!)

Some poets feel comfortable only when writing in rhyme. It is their prop, the means by which a poem can be controlled. And, of course, there are countless superb poems where rhyme is an essential ingredient.

For many, the appeal of poetry is that it involves the making and repetition of verbal patterns and, often, these patterns are based upon rhyme schemes.

There is a challenge to find a rhyme which not only matches in sound the word with which it is paired but also is right with regard to rhythm and meaning and in the context of the poem as a whole, can bring great satisfaction.

Rhyme like meter and other poetic devices needs to enhance the poem's message and not be the main feature. The rhymes should be unobtrusive and add to the musicality of the piece.

299

What is rhyme?

Rhyme is a connection between the sound of syllables not words. In rhyme you use your ear more than your eye.

The two syllables rhyme perfectly because the syllable sounds are identical like *wear/chair*. The spelling is different, but the sound is identical. The consonant sounds after the vowel – if there are any, are identical. *wear /chair*. The syllables begin differently. *Wear/chair.*

The fact that the syllables begin differently is an important characteristic of rhyme because rhyme works by a basic musical principle tension and resolution.

Difference moving to sameness – our ears or brains pick up the sound difference and tune in to the two sounds being alike.

Thus, sound tension and sound resolution make the perfect chime. Our ear likes patterns, so those identical chimes stand out our brain waits for them. If a syllable does not start off sounding different our ear hears repetition, not rhyme.

Rhyme works on a *difference* then a *similarity*; without that there will be no perfect rhyme. Tension and resolution of sound.

Internal Rhyme

Rhyming does not just have to be at the end of lines.

Internal rhyme will also give the same pleasant sound repetition.

Example of internal rhyme:

*The hideaway down the hill. - my **retreat***

*So hard to **beat** the views spill.*

*Vote for **me,** I have charisma, **pedigree.***

What is perfect rhyme?

A rhyme is a repetition of similar sounds (or the same sound) in two or more syllables in lines in poems and songs.

Two words rhyme if their **STRESSED VOWEL** (syllable) and all following **SOUNDS** are identical.

Two lines of poetry rhyme if their final strong positions are filled with rhyming words.

A rhyme in the strict sense is also called a perfect rhyme.

When we use perfect rhyme, we get tension and resolution in the sounds.

Examples are:

sight and *flight*,

deign and *gain*,

madness and *sadness*.

Note it is the **SOUNDS,** not the **SPELLING.**

Types of perfect rhyme:

When two words rhyme as single syllables, the result is said to be a "masculine" rhyme: usually one syllable words although multisyllable words that have the stress on the last syllable are also masculine rhymes.

noun – town

rare - despair

When two words have two syllables or more, the resultant rhyme is said to be a "feminine" rhyme: Here the rhyme is on the *oss* plus the *ing*.

CROSS/ing - TOSS/ing

Here the *ict* plus the *or* make the rhyme it must be the stressed syllable making the rhyme.

VICT/or - preDIC/tor

Note: It must be **THE STRESSED SYLLABLE** that rhymes not just the final syllable in feminine rhymes. The stressed syllable is often the penultimate syllable. The stressed syllable and all following sounds.

WAG/gle - HAG/gle

NIGHT - to/NIGHT

to/NIGHT - de/LIGHT

se/CURE - as/SURE

Feminine rhymes are hard. Check these words for rhyme when you are using them:

BEAUT/y and *GAI/e/ty* are not a perfect rhyme because the stressed syllables do not sound the same.

SANC/tion and *FRAC/tion* are not a perfect rhyme; the stressed syllables do not sound the same even though the final syllables do.

HARD and *re/WARD* are not a perfect rhyme. the *ard* in *hard* sounds like *hahrd. Ward* in *reward* sounds like *wawrd.*

I see people mostly having difficulty with forced rhyme or feminine rhyme where they rhyme on the wrong syllable.

Rhyme is great if it is done well but dire if done badly.

Examples of perfect rhyme in poetry:

Vital Spark is part of a sonnet written in **iambic pentamete**r using an *abab, cdcd* rhyme scheme:

Vital Spark

The composition sets a vital spark

The artist's hand unseen, forever hid

This study blazing, shaded red to dark

With waves of passion - artist's eye undid

She sits immortalised inside the frame

A picture frozen cold but feeling warm

The tones depict his love connects the flame

The artist holds an image to transform.

304

This sonnet is fully rhymed verse. We have a mix of syllable counts within the rhymes. The stresses on *unhid* and *transform* are on the final syllables making all the rhymes in these stanzas masculine rhyme.

In **Poetic Perfection**, the poet has used feminine rhyme and kept the same rhyme sound all the way through. This is called *monorhyme*. Rhyme is on the penultimate syllable and all following sounds. Read this out loud and feel the effects of using the same sounds at the end of each line, do you think this works? Monorhyme has less tension and resolution than perfect rhyme. What do you think?

Is the monorhyme a strong enough rhythm or would the poem have been more effective with more varied rhyme?

Poetic Perfection by Cathy McCormick

i tried so hard to reach perfection

i strived to make a good selection

i used my powers of detection

some poems (1 syllable!) *i thought had great infection*

and certainly, could use correction

they just did not have good inflection!

bad verse, good verse, which intersection?

i don't dare try to use deflection

must be poetic insurrection

rewriting lines in each direction

i tried to make that great connection

i wrote with anger or affection

and still i failed to reach perfection

but i refuse to feel dejection

i've poems (1 syl!) *of sugar, sweet confection*

unspoiled by words such as affliction

bad poems (lol 1 syl) *may still have resurrection!*

Temper Tantrum by Ruby Pond

I blew my lid when things got tough

A battle raged, the fight was rough

A blind attempt, two fisted try

A rip and tear straight through the eye

This shell it left, not quite enough

I blew my lid

Read the examples aloud. Feel the power of the rhymes on the ear. When in doubt with rhyme use a Rhyming Dictionary. It is not cheating; use it as you would any other dictionary.

Perfect Rhyme Exercise:

Here are some rhyming words. Which ones rhyme perfectly? This is for your own amusement.

• Tough, Bough,

• Heard, Thread.

• Heard, Beard.

• Heard, Blurred.

• Heard, third.

- Slough, Through.

- Slough, Enough.

- Slough, chuff.

- Fear, shear.

- Dead, Bead.

- Dead, Red.

- Dead Read.

- Dead, Said.

- Meat, Suite. Answers p. 366

Exercise: Say these words aloud:

birthplace, place, misplace, preplace, displace

Then these words:

face, airspace, race, space, reface, showcase, ace.

Did you focus on the sounds in the first line?

How about the second line? In the second line you have definite similarities; you have tension and resolution and that is what rhyme is all about.

What does Rhyme Do?

End line rhymes are structurally important. When rhymes are at the ends of lines, they are followed by a pause; this allows the line's idea to ring out into that silent moment. It causes a melodic rest; it will sound like other sounds within the stanza, again heightening its significance. A rhyme at the end of a phrase is in the spotlight position; this gives the poet the chance to put important words there. By choosing the best, strongest, end rhymes you can enhance your story potential, the emotion. You can add excitement. Poor choices will waste those valuable positions.

In *Scar Tissue,* let's look at the rhymes:

Begin, skin, disguise, lies, quicken, thicken, me, key. There is an intriguing story already starting to emerge.

Again. In *Counter Song:*

Along, song, between, mean, event. prevent. true, through.

In *Temper Tantrum* again check out the end rhymes:

Tough, rough, try, eye, enough, lid. huff, cuff, did, hid,

These vignettes show the story build up without the meat of the story and demonstrate the importance of the end of lines especially in spotlighting rhymes.

How about these end rhymes? Do they excite you? *Had, glad, me, we.* So far these end rhymes seem bland, there seems less prospect of a story than in the other rhyme sets.

Rhyme also connects ideas. If you choose your words and sounds with care you can get metaphorical connection out of rhymes as well as the sonic hit. If you can find words that have sound and meaning in common that takes your poetry up a level.

Forsake/break, desire/fire.

Exercise:

Find two poems, one that uses the spotlight feature successfully and one less so.

Other types of 'rhyme' you could use in your poetry.

There are several forms of sound repetition that are called rhyme but in poetic terms are not strictly rhyme. They are good sonic devices and can be used to make rhythm in poetry. Particularly if you are writing Free Verse or classic forms that are not asking for rhyme.

Identity rhyme: *Perfect rhyme* needs the sound of the stressed syllable and all following sounds to be the same but the initial sounds different. *In identity rhymes* all sounds are the same. This type of rhyme is considered inferior because you don't get the tension and resolution that you get with perfect rhyme. This gives identity rather than true rhyme.

Eye rhyme: or sight rhyme is a similarity between the spelling not the sound of words. Move and love. Cough bough.

Identical rhyme is repetition of the same word in the rhyming position. If you end two lines with ground to make a rhyme it is repetition rather than rhyme.

Slant rhyme: Assonance and Consonance are types of slant rhyme. As with everything once you understand the rules you may choose to substitute, an identity or identical rhyme for a perfect rhyme if it upholds the structure of your poem better or you need to finish the end of a line with a word that does not have a perfect rhyme.

Rhyme Schemes

Rhyme schemes for classical poetry are set using letters of the alphabet.

So, in a rhyme scheme for a quatrain of *abab*, the first and third lines would rhyme then the second and fourth lines would rhyme together.

Mother moon radiates universal glow - a

Though shadows fall creating pools of darkness - b

World sparkling bright as day it's wounds to show - a

From evil this bright light gives onto starkness – b

In this stanza there is perfect rhyme. Did you notice it is also in iambic pentameter?

Words of love often suppressed

Kindness taken for granted, unexpressed

Presumption of thoughts, norms and dreams

Seems we no longer talk of schemes

Drifting along feather light

Lack of communication lack of fight

312

Forced Rhyme

Forced rhyme manifests in the following scenarios:

- Rearranging a phrase to put the rhyme at the end of the line
- Adding irrelevant information to make a rhyme or extending the line to make the rhyme
- Choosing an inappropriate word to make a rhyme
- Using a tone incompatible with the rest of the poem to get a rhyme
- Writing a line that doesn't mean anything to get a rhyme

Forced rhyme can be found in amateur poetry everywhere you look. Its presence is so pervasive that poetry editors specifically mention 'forced rhyme' as one of the criteria for manuscript rejection and some editors will not even consider rhyming poetry for publication. Forced rhyme occurs in a few different ways.

When the writer is so desperate for a rhyming word that he or she contorts the whole structure of the poem to make a rhyme. The poet may not even realize they are guilty of this practice.

Here are some examples of forced rhyme:

Meeting her was well timed

It made my heart rhymed

Meeting her was well timed

My heart was truly crimed

Of all the words that would have fit the mood of the first line, why would I choose the word *rhymed*? Because I didn't spend the time to choose a more appropriate end rhyme. The second line had to be inverted in order to fit the rhyme and rhythmic structure. Therefore, it is called *forced* rhyme. All that force is used to make a round word fit into a square line, and it still sounds ridiculous and trite.

Whenever we go out and chalk

with you I like to talk.

You would never say *"with you I like to talk"*. Instead, you would say *"I like to talk with you"*. And yet, some poets will write this unnatural way in order to force the lines to rhyme.

I love you more every day that I live.

For you my life I would give.

This is how Yoda from *Star Wars* speaks.

"Truly wonderful the mind of a child is"

"When nine hundred years old you reach, look as good you will not."

Cute, but not the stuff for a world-renowned piece of poetry.

This life is diverse.

Living on a speck of dust in this universe.

I rode to battle on my beautiful horse,

My promise to bring peace to the land, even by force.

Here the second lines are extended to make the rhyme.

Then you have wrenched rhymes:

Conundrums and conscience's plight,

Who decides if the vision's right.

Where the spelling and sound of the end syllables are the same, but the stressed syllable are different. This can happen when rhyming monosyllable words with multisyllable words.

This happens a lot with words with the suffix *-ing*, where you can get a chime but not a rhyme.

"I sing a train of heart as I do write."

King - AGing - the rhyme is on the *AG* not the *ing*.

315

Ping - GOing - the rhyme is on the *GO* not the *ing*

Whenever you finish a poem, it's a good idea to read it over several times and ask yourself if any of the rhymes are forced. And be honest with yourself! It's easy to let a forced rhyme remain in your poem because you don't want to go to the trouble of rewriting it. On the other hand, if you make the effort and eliminate all forced rhymes from the poem, you (and your readers) will be glad you did.

To learn the nuances of good rhyme you need to become conscious of how you are using rhyme in your work.

Spend some time reading good poetry where you can see rhyme used well, classical forms are good places to see rhyming working at its best. Read poetry critically, look for forced rhyme and learn from that.

Consider what underlying sentiment you are trying to express in rhyme and find more appropriate words that will work. Consult a 'rhyming dictionary' if you cannot think of any other way to phrase your lines.

In defence of rhyme by Samantha Beardon

Poetry is the strangest beast,

with various forms and tools

Including different meters

and different, varying rules

Haiku, Tanka from the East

The syllable count, will never cease

Stanza, sonnet, prose or rhyme

a cornucopia a veritable feast

Maybe I am simple, yes I definitely am

I need to get mind pictures, not take an exam

Poetry needs to speak to elicit a reaction

We all react to different stimuli, get our satisfaction

From high ascetic to hoi polloi

Something will grab us, gasp, laugh or cry

Poets try to paint, pictures in the sky

Using words and concepts,

as they do their best to fly

To entertain, to educate

or maybe distain

317

The audience they hope to attract

and maybe entertain

Humour, concepts, truth and light

Poets write with all their might.

Look at the different rhyme methods in this piece and see what you can identify.

Could you improve those end rhymes?

Family Rhyme — Imperfect Rhyme

Using rhyme families effectively can help you not only move through a poem, but add nuances to the rhythm, melody and feel or tone imparted.

There are several types of rhymes: perfect rhyme and imperfect rhyme or family rhymes (rhyme families). Slant rhyme, eye rhyme and a few others. We are just going to concentrate on perfect and family rhyme.

Perfect rhymes are words whose: (1) stressed syllable vowel sounds are the same, (2) consonant sounds after the vowels are the same if there are any, and (3) the sounds before the vowels are different. **Example:** *cone, bone* or *racket, jacket.*

Imperfect rhymes, or **family rhymes**, are words whose: (1) syllable vowel sounds are the same, (2) consonant sounds after the vowels belong to the same phonetic family, and (3) the sounds before the vowels are different. **Example:** *shut, flood* or *break, cage.*

Using Rhyme Families When You Write

So how did I know *'g'* could be substituted for *'k'* to make a rhyme in *break* and *cage*?

Consonants in language are broken into four groups: depending on how we say them.

319

1.   **plosives**, are stop consonants, explosions of sound, like drums if you think of a noise component in music *(b, d, g, t)*;

2.   **fricatives**, which are like shakers *(v, z)*;

3.   **sibilants**, which are like cymbals and sound like a hissing noise *(f, th, s)*

4.   **nasals**, which resonate from the nasal cavity *(m, n, ng)*.

If you were to put the consonants in a chart to help you navigate the rhyming families, it would look like this:

	Plosives	**Fricatives**	**Nasals**
Voiced	*b d g*	*v TH z zh j*	*m n ng*
Unvoiced	*p t k*	*f th s sh ch*	

The easiest way to use the chart is to first look up a perfect rhyme in your rhyming dictionary, and then move to the sounds within the same family. If you have an end consonant of a *d*, a voiced plosive, you could try rhymes with end consonants *b* and *g*. If you still didn't find the word you wanted you could move to the unvoiced plosives *p,t,k*.

The closer you stay to the family you started in, the better the rhyme will sound – i.e., not forced.

Shut - mutt, cut, slut. Perfect rhymes.

Short *u* sound with *t – t* is an unvoiced plosive so we could look at *p, k* or *b, d, g* for family rhymes.

So using *up* to make a rhyme it could be *cup, tup,* or if using *ud*, it could be *cud, flood, blood*.

Using this system, you could pair *mud* and *rug, mud* and *club,* mud and *grub*.

If you rhyme the words you get partial resolution and a definite chime; not as strong a link as perfect rhyme but enough similarity for your ears to pick up. In English there are groups of words that do not have perfect rhyme so you either make a choice to rethink the diction or go with imperfect rhyme.

If you haven't got to use perfect rhyme but you want some unusual sonic effects, then family rhymes are a good option.

With poetry you have to rely on your words and their sounds to create all the melody. Instead of looking at other poets let's look at some songs that are also poetry.

Being able to use family rhyme will open up how you approach a poem and lead you to a richer experience.

Good rhyme is fabulous; rhyme done badly is horrendous. When you are into your poetic journey you will need to take time to really understand the various types of rhyme.

If you are a poet who loves to rhyme, this is an early task for you.

Another great example of a unique rhymer is Kacey Musgraves, the singer and her close rhyme in *Merry Go Round is* worth studying.

How do you find family rhymes in a rhyming dictionary?

The easiest way to use the chart is to first look up a perfect rhyme in your rhyming dictionary, and then move to the sounds within the same family.

So, if you have an end consonant of *b*, a voiced plosive, once you've tried *d* and *g* , as an end consonant, move to the unvoiced plosives. The closer you stay to the family you started in, the better the rhyme will sound – i.e., not forced.

Additive rhyme.

There is another set of words that do not fit into family rhyme. Words that don't end in consonants.

The word *free*, the word *go*, the word *play*, end in vowel sounds. When we're dealing with open vowels, that is vowels that end the word, or when we're dealing with *l* and *r*, we have to work another way to find opportunities for something less stable than perfect rhyme in the way of sound but that still give a sonic.

In *additive* rhyme, you have two words or two syllables; the second of which adds something that the first doesn't contain. If we wanted a more stable rhyme, we would try to add as little sound as possible to the second member of the pair. We might have *cry* and the only word that would fit our meaning is a word that rhymes with *cry*. Using the long *I* vowel sound, *cry*, what would be the least possible sound that you could add? Think about that for a minute.

Look at the consonants. Look at your family rhyme chart. What are the possibilities? Look at *cry*, *bribe*, using the voice close to *b* or *cry*, *ride*, using the voice close to *d*. *G* is not going to work, just because of the nature of *g*, raising your tongue up and changing the vowel sound. So that here, additively, adding the

323

least possible sound gives us the most stable possibility. Whereas adding extra sounds creates a less stable connection like *cry, smile, cry, bride.* You can move more toward fully resolved or more toward less resolved depending on how much sound you add.

Other examples of additive rhyme:

Go – alone. Free – breeze, cry bride

The kites fly free

As they lift to catch the breeze

Classical Poetry Forms

In this book I can only give you a brief overview of some of the classical forms; to write in depth would be another book. The forms I am introducing you to have enough detail for you to write some test poems. I would recommend if you intend to continue to develop the forms you should do more in depth reading.

Sonnet - Accentual syllabic form.

The sonnet was created around the thirteenth century in Italy, and its name means "little song". It is a lyric poem of fourteen lines, which may follow any of a variety of different rhyming schemes. There are a variety of different types of sonnets (e.g. Italian sonnet, Elizabethan or Shakespearean Sonnet).

The Shakespearean sonnet has a rhyme scheme *of*

A-B-A-B-C-D-C-D-E-F-E-F-G-G.

Note that the two last lines are a rhyming couplet.

This is the place where the poet wraps up the poem - where the story reaches its conclusion.

The **Petrarchan sonnet**, named after the Roman poet Petrarch, consists of an octave (eight-line stanza), rhyming *A-B-B-A-A-B-B-A*, and a sestet (six-line stanza), with the rhyming pattern of *C-D-C-D-C-D*.

The **Spenserian sonnet,** attributed to Edmund
Spencer rhymes thus:

A-B-A-B-B-C-B-C-C-D-C-D E-E.

All Sonnets are metred and usually written in Iambic
Pentameter. In a sonnet there is usually a turn or
change called a *Volta.* In a Shakespearean sonnet
before the final couplet, in a Petrarchan between the
octet and sestet.

Writing sonnets is a skill that will require you to
concentrate on the flow and rhythm of your writing.
The creation of a sonnet is straight forward. The
sonnet is usually associated with love poems, or
tragedies, but if you are creative, you can make the
metered rhymes fit any genre at all.

When I tackle a classical form, I always make up a
stress chart to help me get the words and stresses and
rhymes to match.

Your poem should have a single focus, each stanza of
the sonnet should develop the idea further. Think of
each quatrain as a little thought bubble, like a
paragraph, in which you explore an element of the
subject of your poem. Each quatrain should build
toward the final couplet, where you will have a turn,
or a volta. The turn, which occurs in the 13th line of

326

the Shakespearean sonnet, offers a resolution or insight into to the problem developed in the first three quatrains.

(*a*) × /| × / | × / | × / | × /

(*b*) × /| × / | × / | × / | × /

(*a*) × /| × / | × / | × / | × /

(*b*) × /| × / | × / | × / | × /

(*c*) × /| × / | × / | × / | × /

(*d*) × /| × / | × / | × / | × /

(*c*) × /| × / | × / | × / | × /

(*d*) × /| × / | × / | × / | × /

(*e*) × /| × / | × / | × / | × /

(*f*) × /| × / | × / | × / | × /

(*e*) × /| × / | × / | × / | × /

(*f*) × /| × / | × / | × / | × /

(*g*) × /| × / | × / | × / | × /

(*g*) × /| × / | × / | × / | × /

Scheme example for a Shakespeare Sonnet,

A Spenserian Sonnet by Christopher Buckley.

On Wings, a Prayer

In youth it was the soundboard for her hand,

with strings that lent her inner voice a strain.

She'd hold it gently as her fingers fanned,

they'd trail her joyous heart; those notes a train.

But then a thing I never will explain;

for gardens it now graces, as she's passed:

no rationale for hearing the refrains,

of ones she loved and harped until her last.

I thought perhaps the angels were broadcast.

Legatos in the breezes swept errant.

She plucking still where ghosts of she were cast?

Not so, but maybe near as aberrant:

The bees that played with petals while on wing,

caressed too tautened gut and made it sing...

See **Vital Spark** (p56) for a Shakespearean Sonnet.

328

La'Tuin Accentual syllabic form.

See **Pitter Patter** by Miriam Ruff, on page 45

The La'Tuin, a poetic form created by Laura Lamarca, consists of 4-line stanzas with an *ABCA ABCA* rhyme scheme that is consistent throughout each stanza. Stanzas 2, 3, etc. must all follow the same rhyme sounds as the first stanza. With the first stanza being repeated again at the end of the piece. It contains a minimum of 4 stanzas, with no maximum length limit.

A strict syllable count of 9/8/9/8 is required per stanza.

In-Depth Explanation of rhyme:

Lines 1, 4, 5, 8, 9, 12, 13, 16 etc., all rhyme - this is the 'A' rhyme.
Lines 2, 6, 10, 14 etc, all rhyme - this is the 'B' rhyme.
Lines 3, 7, 11, 15 etc, all rhyme - this is the 'C' rhyme.

The La'Tuin is named after A'Tuin, a giant turtle

from the *Diskworld* series. A turtle is a symbol of Mother Earth. La is Laura Lamarca's signature.

Free Verse - poetry that is based on the irregular rhythmic cadence recurring, with variations of phrases, images, and syntactical patterns rather than the conventional use of meter. In other words, free verse has no rhythm scheme or pattern. However, much poetic language and devices are found in free verse. Rhyme may or may not be used in free verse, but, when rhyme is used, it is used with great freedom. In other words, free verse has no rhyme scheme or pattern. Free verse does not mean rhyme cannot be used, only that it must be used without any pattern.

Free verse is a challenging form that utilizes the natural cadences of common speech to create rhythm in lieu of the strict usage of meter found in classic forms. Free verse is the breaking of some old rules and the utilization of new tools, not the elimination of any and all rules.

Free verse often uses the natural cadence of speech to determine the length of each line in order to bring each new thought to its natural end or pause. The tools used to do this are the line stop established by punctuation, or enjambment, or inserting a strategic line break. Enjambment must have purpose and is not to be arbitrarily employed. It should be used to pull the reader through a short line to the next, where the thought can end on a weighty word capable of making the reader pause to absorb what has just been said. Or it will cause the line to end on an article (so on the following line be sure to use a word with some weight that can carry the reader through to the natural stop). When used skilfully, enjambment will not only carry the reader's attention through the poem but will create tension in the piece that complements the connotations, imagery, or metaphors intended by the author. You will find many Free Verse examples in the *Let's Read Poetry* chapter.

Haiku - Syllabic Form. A Japanese poem composed of three unrhymed lines of five, seven, and five morae (sounds), usually written in less than 14 syllables in English. Often related to nature or the seasons. These are lyrical poems framed in a moment in time; an image then a comment in the form of a second image. Nearly every Haiku is an attempt make us consider ordinary experiences in a poetic and extra-ordinary way.

Please see the *Tanka* explanation about Japanese sounds which will affect the information you will see about how to write Haiku in many places.

In modern thinking, Haiku are written in 3 lines of short, long, short syllables and written in 14 syllables or less. You need to read Haiku from verified sources to understand how to write the perfect Haiku. A Haiku is untitled and has no punctuation other than an *em dash* or *ellipsis* sometimes.

day break -
the fleeting shadow from
an eagles wing

spring breeze
the new-born lambs
first breath

Tanka - Syllabic Form. A five-line lyric poem from Japan. It is an unrhymed syllabic form. Tanka is grounded in concrete imagery but infused with lyricism and intimacy, there is the most amazing chance to charge this small gem with emotion. This is achieved by direct expression, suggestion and nuance. You have already encountered Tanka in the book.

The biggest issue with Tanka is how it is portrayed for English speaking poets. In Japan the Tanka is written in phrases of 5, 7, 5 morae or sounds. The Japanese do not have syllables in their language they use sounds; these do not directly equate to English syllables but when Tanka were first written in

English they were written in strict 5, 7, 5 syllables and you will find much information on the internet using this format. You can still use it but it makes for a heavy poem compared to the Japanese poem. If you look on the website of the American Tanka Society or other specialist Tanka organisations you will see the advice is different.

The suggestion is Tanka is written in less than 31 syllables, an optimum of 22 or less, but the syllable count is less important than getting the essence of Tanka right. It should be written in lines of a short-long-short-long-long structure.

To become familiar with Tanka and how to write them you need to read widely of good Tanka. There are many good journals out there. Tanka are difficult to write well but amazing when the spark happens.

a hummingbird
sips nectar the colour
of sunset . . .
the sweet & sour of spending
each evening on my own

The Triolet: An eight-line poem. Of French origin emphasising repetition and rhyme.

It has two refrains that run throughout with two rhymes.

1.   A

2.   B

3.   a Rhymes with 1st line.

4.   A identical to 1st line.

5.   a Rhymes with 1st line.

6.   b Rhymes with 2nd line.

7.   A Identical to 1st line.

8.   B Identical to 2nd line.

Note that the lst, 4th, and 7th lines are identical. The 2nd and 8th lines are identical. Lines 3, 5, 6 are single, different.

The rhyme scheme, ABaAabAB, can be in iambic tetrameter or iambic pentameter.

A reminder of the metre terms:

Iambic pentameter is 10 syllables per line ...unstressed then stressed.

Iambic tetrameter is 8 syllables per line ...unstressed then stressed.

Triolet can be written as one-line poem or combined to make a corona of two, three or four linked Triolets.

OCEAN LINER TRIOLET by David Bray

Stately great ocean liner steaming

To distant horizons afar

On the bridge, her brass all gleaming

Stately great ocean liner steaming

Down below her turbines screaming

navigating by a star

Stately great ocean liner steaming

To distant horizons afar

Villanelle: This is arguably one of the strongest repeating refrain forms in classical poetry. An Italian folk song developed into a poetry form by the French.

Its use of two alternating refrains creates an echo that reverberates throughout its nineteen lines. The result is an intensity that can be both haunting and powerful; it is this intensity that leads the villanelle to most often be used in the dramatic creation of strong emotions, or deeply emotional themes.

There is a limited rhyming scheme, just two rhymes are used with two refrain lines. The poem is comprised of six stanzas: five tercets followed by a single quatrain, each of which uses at least one of the refrain lines, in alternating sequence.

Here is the basic pattern, using A1 for the first refrain, A2 for the second, and (a) and (b) for the other lines. Each stanza is shown on a single line here, but is made of individual lines in the poem:

Stanza 1:   A1, b, A2

Stanza 2:   a, b, A1

Stanza 3:   a, b, A2

Stanza 4:   a, b, A1

Stanza 5:   a, b, A2

Stanza 6:   a, b, A1, A2.

Metre is not compulsory, but many poets use iambic pentameter with the form.

See *Do not Go Gentle that Good Night* by Dylan Thomas.

Villanelle by W.H. Auden

One Art by Elizabeth Bishop.

Crafting a villanelle presents us with some challenges. The first, and most important, is to choose a meter and create your main couplet that forms the refrains. These two lines will echo throughout the body of the poem. They must work together, in both your opening stanza as well as the final statement in the ending quatrain. These two lines must also stand alone, as the final line in each tercet stanza along the way. Once you have decided on a topic then you must find that strong couplet and good rhymes.

Overleaf is a Villanelle under construction it needs work yet on metre and rhyme. Look at it and find the glitches that need sorting.

You became a megabyte of madness

Since we met, life's never been the same

We frankly share happiness and sadness

No false catechism staunches blackness

We truly listen and do not shame

You became a megabyte of madness

We share our secrets with a gladness

Shake our heads with respect but never blame

We frankly share happiness and sadness

Friends across the ether, so priceless

Fate introduced us on a word game

You became a megabyte of madness

We highlight most of our flaws, with bluntness

But you cheer me when my world is aflame

We frankly share happiness and sadness

To say we are in love would be baseless

A different emotion we sustain

You became a megabyte of madness

We frankly share happiness and sadness

338

Kyrielle is a French form of rhyming poetry written in quatrains (a stanza consisting of 4 lines), and each quatrain contains a repeating line or phrase as a refrain (usually appearing as the last line of each stanza). Each line within the poem consists of only eight syllables. There is no limit to the number of stanzas a Kyrielle may have, but three is considered the accepted minimum.

Some popular rhyming schemes for a Kyrielle are: *aabB, ccbB, ddbB,* with *B* being the repeated line, or *abaB, cbcB, dbdB.* Mixing up the rhyme scheme is possible for an unusual pattern of: *axaZ, bxbZ, czcZ, dxdZ,* etc. with *Z* being the repeated line. The rhyme pattern is completely up to the poet.

Heartfelt Words (kyrielle) by Miriam Ruff

The words don't want to come today
They slip out from my mental grasp
I know just what I want to say
My heart is lonely, take me back

I dive into the depths of hell
My fingers reaching out to clasp
The words of love drowned in the well
My heart is lonely, take me back

Will they return to me some day
Their absence makes all light turn black
I need the words to make you stay
My heart is lonely, take me back

I'm sorry for the pain I've caused
Emotions raw, the soul they rasp
I need my words to make you pause
My heart is lonely, take me back

Loop Poem*:*   Loosely, a loop poem can pertain to
any type of poem, there are no rules on length or
rhyme or meter, only that for each stanza or verse,
the last word of a line becomes the first word of the
next line and the last word of that line becomes the
first word of the following line, and the pattern
repeats until the last line where the final word will be
the first line of the poem. Patterns are repeated
repeated within loops loops that keep repeating
repeating all these patterns.

Patterns are repeated
repeated within loops
loops that keep repeating
repeating all these patterns.

Rondeau. A 13th century French form originally sung.

The rondeau's form is not difficult to recognize; it is composed of fifteen lines of eight to ten syllables each, divided stanzaically into a quintet, a quatrain, and a sestet. The refrain consists of the first few words or the entire first line of the first stanza, and it recurs as the last line of both the second and third stanzas. Two rhymes guide the music of the rondeau, whose rhyme scheme is as follows (R representing the refrain): *aabba aabR aabbaR.*

The challenge of writing a rondeau is finding an opening line worth repeating and choosing two rhyme sounds that offer enough word choices. Modern Rondeaus are often playful.

Double Dactyl. A dactyl is a triple-syllable foot, with the stress on the first syllable (screwdriver, marmalade).

A double dactyl is a pairing (higgledy-piggledy).

Double dactyl verse form consists of two four-line stanzas, the first three lines of each is a double dactyl. The last lines of each verse consist of a dactyl and a single syllable. Last words of each stanza to rhyme.

Other rules-

First line to be nonsense

341

Second line to be the subject of the poem, with a proper-name noun

Third line of either verse to be a single six-syllable double dactyl

Most published examples follow the rules somewhat loosely!

Example of a Double Dactyl

Voluminosity by David Bray

Chompingly chewingly

Cheese pies and baconly

enthusiastically

middle-aged spread

Rumbelly-tumbelley

hunger pangs gnawingly

polyunsaturate

kilos to shed

Editing a poem condensing the message

Revising your poem and tightening the flow is important.

The following is a blueprint for the editing process:

Make a copy of the poem and do your analysis on the copy; then you always have the original. This way you can always revert if your changes don't work as you hoped.

Read your poem aloud, slowly; feel the rhythm, the flow, the glitches.

Here are the first three things to consider:

Is there enough use and variation of images in the poem?

Would this work better in another viewpoint –

1st person *(I)* or 2nd *(the instruction model)* or 3rd *(He, she)* ?

Are there any clichés that need changing?

The next part of the edit needs doing sequentially; the order is important. Don't rush the process.

Read every stanza – is it needed, or just there for colour, or a digression, or comment or repetition of an idea already stated? Can it be removed without loss?

Think about every line, is it a comment or central to moving the poem on? Can it be removed without loss?

Consider every word, do you need the connectives (*and, the, those, this* etc.). Can they be removed without loss?

Are identifiers used too often (*Fred said*, or *he said*)? Can these be replaced with a pronoun *(he, she, it, them)*?

Do you need to identify an action with a pronoun or a name label?

A golden rule is – If you are not sure about something, remove it.

Consider any adjectives – are they adding anything or are they just for colour? If so, do I need that colour? (Avoid more than one adjective with a noun).

Your verbs – have you used the base form of the verb? If not, consider changing to the base form. Edit the line as required to change the verb.

What are your adverbs doing? Using an adverb as a modifier. If so, is there a better verb to use?

Is the tense *(was/is)* and number *(they/it)* consistent?

Is there a more obvious form or shape for this poem?

Revisit the title. Is it saying too much or too little? Is there a better title?

Finally read the poem over aloud, pause at each line ending, listen to it and consider if all parts are working together.

Now you can relax. Smile. Your work is done. It's the best poem you have written. It's time to get it out there and wow the world........

NOW is the time to wait! You may find there is further work to be done.

So, leave it now, put it away and wait until the euphoria has settled. If you can't wait that long show it to a poet whose judgement you trust. But a week or two of relaxation in your notebook or on your computer will allow your poem to mature. At least it will allow the rosy glow to dissipate then you can read it afresh; perhaps you will see a new perspective.

We know that all the great poets revised their poems. There are examples of poems before and after revision. There is evidence that Elizabeth Bishop took many months to complete a poem and that she left blanks in lines until she could find the perfect word.

How to move your poetry forward. Once you are comfortable with poetic techniques, practice. Find yourself a mentor somebody you trust who has good poetic skills and ask for feedback on a few of your best poems. Do not presume, and do not overload the other person with work. They too will be working poets.

Start to read other poets work critically and learn.

346

Journeys End by Laurie Grove

The day narrows into dusk.

Fireflies strike their tinders

To guide the last straggling rays

Of light as they nestle down

Through the trees, looking

For a bed for the night.

A single wind turbine stands silent

On top of the hill, arms out wide;

Much like one who once suffered

On another hill a long time ago.

A stream runs down to the woods;

Every splash and ripple plays

Through the undergrowth; its music

Orchestrated by wind and guesswork.

Night soon falls; early rising stars

Yawn and rub sleep from their eyes

As they wake and shuffle into

Position; blind moles peak out,

Snouting for earthworms up for air.

The first bat squawks, testing its sonar.

Owls preen tail feathers ready to hunt,

As the woodland loam shivers

At the hint of a night-frost to come

She has come far; the horns,

Barks and pounding hooves,

Long behind her. She can rest;

let her body ease back

Into rhythm and shape;

Wrap herself in the comfort

Of her brush and sleep.

She enters the safety of shadows,

Padding light and dainty,

Foxy lady; you are home

Here is a critique of this piece by David John Terelinck.

"I truly love this poem, and it is one of a rare few where I say, "damn, wish I'd written that." Wish I could put my name to it. Annoyed you wrote it, and I didn't! But only for a second, and delighted you penned this. What a read!

This is sensitively written and is so rich with imagery and unstated emotion. I feel I am there as the sun is setting and the night is coming alive. I am seeing what this fox is seeing as she seeks shelter and safety of night and wood. What thrills me about this is the freshness of the writing. It feels authentic as if the poet has been to the wood he is writing about. You unfold a narrative with all showing, not an ounce of tell. And the narrator does not intrude for a second. There is much to enjoy in this, and some of the things that stand out for me are:

~ the metaphor that compares the wind turbine to the crucifixion is STUNNING. So original!

~ love *the stars yawning* . . . can really picture this as the sky darkens and they grow bright like a mouth opening in the blackness. And I think it is great how they *"shuffle into / Position"* – inspired writing

~ *the woodland loam shivers in anticipation of the frost* is delicious personification; great writing

~ and the ending inspired . . . the sensual allusion of nature to femininity. And the respite after the chase

~ and the easing back into rhythm and shape says so much about how this fox has been stretched beyond her limits to escape

All of this poem excites me. And it attracts me because of its very simplicity. It is well written with everyday language but constructed in an extraordinary way that it really sings. The way you string words together in original ways means you don't have to try and be clever with big words and confounding lines. You use imagery and metaphor to paint an unmistakable picture. Not an ounce of confusion or abstraction in this; just real writing and poetic discourse.

The rhythm and pace are lovely; nothing trips the tongue when this is recited aloud. Stanzas are tight and I cannot see any superfluous words employed. I can honestly say this is one of the best poems you have ever written. And I do know I have been scathing and critical at times – of you and others –

bur praise where praise is due . . . this IS poetry . . .
REAL POETRY that speaks to me as a reader.

As I said, I wish I had this one under my belt. It's a
keeper, and I hope more people get to enjoy it as
well."

LAST WORD

We have reached our journeys end. The end of a
foray into the realm of poetry from the perspective of
the tools we as poets have at our disposal, and live
examples of poems to test your learning. The trouble
with looking at figurative language, word choice,
rhythm and metre as separate entities is that in a
poem, they all work together. The poem is the
synchronisation of all the elements of poetic theory
into the perfect exciting read.

I hope this book has opened possibilities for you, that
you have a vision of the craft of the poet.

Necessarily this book has not covered all aspects of
rhetoric, poetic devices or figurative language. The
glossary is a partial glossary of the terms you could
come across. However, this book covers a great deal
of the information that will help you expand your
poetic horizons.

There are many resources available on the internet some good, others ill informed. Use them but use them wisely.

I have tried to research the material carefully and therefore I have provided you with the best information based on experience and learning. Others may see things differently I leave you to continue your journey into poetry. I wish you luck.

Samantha

APPENDICES

Tips for new poets

- It's fine to write straight out of your head if you have an idea.
- It is not fine to then think your work is done.
- After writing, read your work carefully looking for errors.
- Read your work aloud.
- Feel how it flows. Do your words make a stumble as you read? If so, it needs a new word or words to eradicate the stumble.
- Is your meaning clear?
- Is your word choice good? Would a synonym give you better rhythm, better musicality? Diction clear?
- Are there words in your poem that are just window dressing and are not needed?
- Are there adjectives you could remove?
- If you are writing about something unfamiliar, read around the subject first.
- If it's an emotive subject pertinent to the opposite sex, write in the third person. Trying to write in the first person is often patronising.
- Write about what you know; it can make a great poem.

- Try to incorporate the senses into your writing, Sight, hearing, smell, taste, touch. This brings your poem alive
- Don't *tell* you are in love, sad, etc. These are abstract emotions *show* me....
- Its sometimes great to plan your poem or write for 5 minutes and pull out points to make a poem.
- Your readers want to be sitting on your shoulders, seeing what you see, feeling what you feel. They want to be excited and wowed.
- Poetry needs to be authentic, interesting and accessible.

Making words Sing

"Words are, of course, the most powerful drug used by mankind." - Rudyard Kipling, from a speech to the Royal College of Surgeons London 1923.

Words are a poet's medium. Although poetry is often written and read more than spoken and heard it is designed to be spoken, it is designed to be heard. Even if only heard with the inner ear poetry is written for auditory and visual enjoyment.

Poets paint pictures with words, they utilise the full power of words to people their poetry. Meanings, connotations, sounds, chimes, tropes; we use them all.

See them crisp and beautiful on the page surrounded by a sea of white space. Rich tones that quiver and sing.

How can you make your words sing?

Read them out loud. Listen for rhythms and cadence.

Understand and utilise the sounds of syllables.

Understand and utilise speech patterns.

Add in phrases or clauses to slow things down.

Choose words that speed things up because we say them quickly.

355

Add sensory description to increase emotion.

Use repetition to heighten messages.

Change the length of lines to change stability.

Change stanza lengths.

Minimise adverbs and adjectives.

Use metaphors and similes if you want the reader to appreciate the imagery.

Pick the strongest noun, the strongest verb.

Don't start lines with *"There was"* or *"There were."*

Rearrange where the verb and noun are in the line but don't make it passive, lines need to be active.

Add emotion in the verb choice you make and by using sense-bound writing.

Use modern words. Reduce the use of archaic words.

Substitute any *"be"* verb for a verb that's specific and vivacious. You know you've got a good one when you can see exactly what is happening.

Try to substitute every word for a synonym to see what you come up with. Is there a word with better sound quality and connotations?

Don't use big, multi-syllable words for effect; it may muddy your meaning better to keep it simple.

Look for red flags.

Look for weak modifiers like *very* or *some.*

If a word in a line doesn't have a precise purpose, take it out.

Poems that progress and unfold a story are highly valued. Journey within poems engage the reader.

Build your poem and the tension as each stanza unfolds.

Have a powerful and satisfactory closing stanza and lines. Words are our medium. We have control over them. Chose them with care and precision.

When you have written, read, and polished your poems your words will sing, paint glorious pictures and wow your readers.

In words we have a cornucopia of tools to produce poetry that is visceral, vivid, melodious.

How to get your poetry published.

- Read copies of the journals you want to submit to. This gives you a feel for the sort of content they publish; unless exceptionally well-done editors do not like rhyme. Many magazines will not accept it.

- Unless you know the publication likes long poems, keep it short.

- Submit three to five poems in one go never more.

- Make a great eye-catching title.

If you want to publish a poetry pamphlet or a book and you want it to be published by a mainstream publishing house, then you need to have several pieces published in journals before you even bother to submit. The competition is fierce and manuscripts from unknown authors are rarely read.

There are many opportunities to get work published but it takes dedication to research the market. Match up poems to journals and keep a steady stream in the post. Even well-known poets struggle to get more than a handful published a year.

You will also have to develop a pragmatic attitude because you will get many rejections.

Nuggets of wisdom about poetry

'The BEST poetry writers are also dedicated editors of what they write. Great poetry needs to be edited; critically. Gems have little value when pulled from the clay in which they are mined; they need to be polished to have appeal. Poetry is no different. First drafts are only the beginning . . . the raw material.

I believe there is a big difference between being a poet, and just being a typist. Anyone can hit the keyboard and type words on a page to bash out a poem. It doesn't mean it's good. It's the real craftsman that takes the time to hammer those words into shape. Metaphor, simile and structure are the anvil we shape around. It is the editing that makes quality poems. Editing is one of the vital organs of poetry.'

The above from David John Terelinck.

'Having just finished the sonnet challenge, I thought I would share something about how we learn and progress when we are trying to develop a new skill such as poetry writing.

There are four main stages: UI, CI, UA, CA, (although in reality these stages blur into a continuum).

Stage one – UI – Unconscious Inability. We all usually start here. It simply means we are no good at the skill, but we are unaware that we are no good. We may never have tried the skill or are not aware that the skill requires some knowledge or training. Often, we pass through this stage very quickly, once we try the skill and see it is not as easy as we thought. Unfortunately, there are some who do not recognise their limitations or continue to believe that no special effort is required to acquire the skill. Such people will carry on forever in the first stage unaware of their inability.

Stage two – CI – Conscious Inability. Everyone not stuck in stage one enters this stage. It is where we know we a have more to learn but have not yet learnt it. For most this is a natural recognition and is vital if one wants to learn. This is the stage of effort and training. It is the motivation to acquire the skill that sets this stage apart.

Stage three – Unconscious Ability. This is where we have gained some ability and can demonstrate this in our actions but are not yet clear why it seems to work. Many great sports people would be examples of this. They have a natural talent. This is not to say that such people do not practice and try to develop even further but they start with an advantage that the skill just works. However, if it is a skill that has value there is still more learning to be done to reach the final stage.

Stage four - Conscious Ability. This is the stage where one can demonstrate the skill but crucially knows what techniques or knowledge inform how to demonstrate that skill. For everyone, this is the end of a long journey involving time and hard work, and probably many failures. It is also most likely that anyone reaching this stage will be rather humble about saying so, as there is always more to learn.

Applying this to poetry, I think the conclusions are obvious. We can all write stuff that we think is poetry and sometimes it is and sometimes it is not. However, to write good poetry takes effort and practice; and, above all, the humility to receive critical feedback as a means to learn and improve. Nobody knows it all; nobody is above criticism. Everyone can improve, but only if they really want to.'

The above from Laurie Grove of the Rising Moon Poetry Group.

'Writing a poem is about more than getting words down onto paper. Before one can write great poetry, one needs to understand what it is that makes poetry great. And this goes back to one of my harping bugbears . . . budding poets need to read widely and deeply of quality published poetry. This is such a wonderful teacher about style, construction, forms, sound, imagery. Putting words on paper is just typing . . . writing is *making* the words work, it's *how* you put them on the paper.' *David John Terelinck*

Exercise Answers

P 66   Part of a short story

Two stanzas of a poem

An instapoem.

P 124 Identify the assonance

If w*e* m*ee*t on str*ee*t or bus
S*a*y you s*a*w me in the rain
L*i*ke a *little* del*i*cate b*i*rd
A str*o*ng s*o*ng g*o*ne we decline

P140   Agog.

I am bowled over by her beauty

She has an aura around her

untouchable disdainful yet irresistible

yet she walks around inviting love

demanding attention promising

love with her behaviour demanding adoration

she is fickle she wants to subjugate all

but keeps her heart whilst she breaks others

feel free to get involved with her

she will break your heart and turn

you into a sullen zombie

bind you to her be miserable

in your adoration.

P 268 Find the syllables in the following words.

Won/der/ful

Sand

Din/ner

Cal/en/dar

Por/cu/pine

Sneeze

Fire

In *sneeze* and *fire* you have the lazy *e* at the end the
schwa sound.

P 278 Your challenge was to divide this poem into stressed and unstressed syllables.

MI/rage SHIM/mer/ing /in /the/ HEAT/ed AIR
no o/A/sis PRO/ject/ed/on /the/ DE/sert
just/ SHIM/mer/ing/ AIR
i/ CAN/not /TOUCH
an /ab/STRAC/tion
i/DO/ NOT/ un/der/STAND
MI/rage SHIM/mer/ing/ in/the/ HEAT/ed /AIR
No/ o/A/sis/ PRO/ject/ed/on/ the/ DE/sert
JUST/ SHIM/mer/ing /AIR
i/ CAN/not /TOUCH
an /ab/STRAC/tion

P 300 Iambic pentameter lines?

Where green maize fills the fields without sorrow. - No

Ten boats all jostled hard to gauge the line. - Yes

Like ghosts they echo every step I take. – Yes

In autumn's breeze my world began to turn. - Yes

P 309 Perfect Rhyme Exercise - Answers.

Do these words rhyme?

• Tough, Bough	No
• Heard, Thread.	No
• Heard, Beard.	No
• Heard, Blurred.	No
• Heard, third.	Yes
• Slough, Through.	No
• Slough, Enough.	Yes
• Slough, chuff.	Yes
• Fear, shear.	Yes
• Dead, Bead.	No
• Dead, Red.	Yes
• Dead Read.	Yes
• Dead, Said.	Yes
• Meat, Suite.	Yes

Glossary

Accent: the emphasis or stress placed on a syllable in a line of poetry.

Acrostic: Poetry where certain letters, usually the first in each line form a word or message when read in a sequence.

Allegory: One thing representing something else in a poem or other work of art. This works on a literal level but has another meaning.

Alliteration: The repetition of consonants at the beginning of adjacent or closely connected words.

Amphibrach: Di-Dum-Di, a three-syllable foot unstressed, stressed, unstressed syllables.

Anapaest: Di-Di-Dum, a foot with two short syllables before one long:

Assonance: An imperfect form of rhyme which counts only the vowel sound of the chief rhyming syllable. Repetition of the vowel sounds to chime and underline.

Ballad: A narrative poem, orally transmitted and, traditionally, sung. Tells a story similar to a folk tale.

Caesura: A break within the poetic line. In English poetry, this can occur anywhere in the line. It can be achieved by punctuation or extra spaces.

Catalectic: Lacking the last syllable.

Cinquain: A number of poetry forms have the title cinquains they all have in common the five-line form.

Consonance: Repetition of similar or identical consonants where vowels differ. Half rhyme is consonance of the final consonants.

Couplet: A group of two poetic lines, often rhyming.

Dactyl: Dum-di-di, a foot with a trio of stressed, unstressed, unstressed syllables.

Dimeter: A line consisting of two poetic feet.

Dramatic monologue: A type of poem which is spoken to a listener. The speaker addresses a specific topic while the listener unwittingly reveals details about him/herself.

Elegy: A sad and thoughtful poem about the death of an individual.

Ellipsis: Omission of words from a sentence to achieve brevity and compression usually written as three dots ...

End-stopped: An end-stopped line ends with a pause, however brief, sometimes indicated by a punctuation mark.

Enjambment: The running of one line on to the next without a pause.

Envoi: concluding stanza of certain poetry forms such as the Sestina.

Eye rhyme: A rhyme that doesn't rhyme fully but looks as if it should.

Feminine rhyme: The accented syllable in multisyllabic words is the penultimate or antepenultimate:

Foot: In order to understand the construction of a line of verse, we divide it into feet. One iamb equals one foot.

Found poetry: poetry created by taking words, phrases, and

passages from other sources and re-framing them by adding spaces, lines, or by altering the text with additions or subtractions.

Free verse (vers libre): Poetry written in either rhyme or unrhymed lines that have no set fixed metrical pattern.

Heroic couplets: A poem written in pairs of rhymed iambic pentameters is said to be in heroic couplets.

Hexameter: A line of six feet.

Iamb: Di-Dum, a foot of two syllables, the most important unit of English poetry.

Iambic pentameter: One pair of syllables an unstressed syllable followed by one stressed syllable (iamb) five sets in a line.   Di dum, di dum, di dum, di dum, di dum. Used extensively in classical form poetry to give metre.

Line: In modern written poetry, a line may vary in length from List poetry: A poem that is made up of a list of items or events. It can be any length and rhymed or unrhymed

Metaphor: Figurative use of a word or phrase to describe something to which it is not literally applicable. A comparison of different things with a common characteristic.

Metre: metre is a repeating pattern in the lines of a poem, using unstressed and stressed syllables

Metonym: A word or phrase is used to stand in for what it represents: 'the bottle' is a metonym for 'drinking', 'stage' for 'theatrical life', 'the crown' for the monarchy.

Monometer: A metric line of one foot.

Masculine Rhyme: occurs when the rhyme is on the final syllable of the two rhyming words. In one syllable words, masculine rhyme is easy to identify.

Ode: or dirge sung or declaimed by a single individual.

A lengthy lyric poem typically of a serious or meditative nature and having an elevated style and formal stanza structure. Often written to commemorate public events.

Octave: A group of eight lines of poetry, often forming the first part of a sonnet.

Ottava Rima: A poem in eight-line stanzas, rhyming abababcc

Personification: writing about something not human as if it were a person, for example 'The sun smiles at us'

Poetic inversion: reversing the order of normal speech in order to make the words fit a particular rhythm, or rhyme, or both.

Quatrain: group of four lines of poetry, usually rhymed.

Refrain: a line or phrase repeated throughout a poem, sometimes with variations, often at the end of each stanza.

Pastoral: A poem that depicts rural life in a peaceful, romanticized way.

Quatrain: A stanza or poem consisting of four lines. Lines 2 and 4 must rhyme while having a similar number of syllables.

Rondeau: A lyrical poem of French origin having 10 or 13

lines with two rhymes and with the opening phrase

repeated twice as the refrain,

Senryu: A short Japanese style poem, like haiku in structure that treats human beings rather than nature: Often in a humorous or satiric way.

Sestet: The last six lines of a sonnet.

Sestina: A poem consisting of six six-line stanzas and a three-line envoy. The end words of the first stanza are repeated in varied order as end words in the other stanzas and also recur in the envoy.

Tanka: A Japanese poem of five lines, unrhymed syllabic. High in Imagery

Tetrameter: A line of four feet.

Tercet: A verse of three lines.

Terza Rima: A type of poetry consisting of 10 or 11 syllable lines arranged in three-line tercets.

Triplet: A group of three poetic lines, often rhyming, as for instance the tercet.

Trochee: Dum-di. A two-syllable foot, the reverse of the iamb stressed and unstressed syllable.

Trope: A figurative use of an expression or word. The repetition of a theme such as a motif.

Villanelle: A 19-1ine poem consisting of five tercets and a final quatrain on two rhymes. The first and third lines of the first tercet repeat alternately as a refrain closing the succeeding stanzas and joined as the final couplet of the quatrain

This is of necessity a truncated glossary - go out and explore the language of poetry.

Recommended Reading

There are so many poetry books out there to explore here are some you might find interesting. These are my "go to" collections:

Taking Off Emily Dickinson's Clothes – Billy Collins (Anything by Billy Collins is worth looking up.)

Treasures of the Damned – Charles Bukowski (Harsh poetry but very influential)

Collected Poems – *Adrian Henri* (poetry from the 60's in Liverpool)

Worlds – Penguin Books.

Writing Poems – Peter S Sansom.

Rhymes Reasons – John Hollander.

The Making of a Poem, A Norton Anthology of Poetic Forms – Mark Strand and Eaven Boland.

*The Ode Less Travelle*d – Stephen Fry.

And if you want to know what makes a perfect pamphlet, I recommend:

Like a Fish Out of Batter – Catherine Graham (Indigo Dreams)

Ten Windows Transform the World - Jane Hirshfield.

40 Sonnets- Don Patterson

The Practice of Poetry. - Robin Behen and Chase Twitchell.

Serious Concern -. Wendy Cope

There is a myriad of Internet Resources such as:

The Poetry Foundation: www.poetryfoundation.org

The Tanka Society of America:
www. Tankasocietyofamerica.org

Poetry Society of America

Contributors of Poems to the book.

Susannah Bailey is the pseudonym of Beth who grew up in the UK and now lives in Sydney, Australia. A lifelong love of words has led her to writing poetry, and recently she had a tanka sequence accepted by the International Tanka Society. She enjoys exploring different forms of poetry and is a constant reader.

RubyPond is a poet and fiction author with works published in Rhetoric Askew anthologies, Stitch Smile Publications and currently working on a novel. She lives in Jacksonville Florida.

David Terelinck is an Australian poet living on the Gold Coast in Queensland, Australia. In another lifetime he had been involved in academic writing and has had many articles published in peer-reviewed nursing journals Recently, after 10 years devoted to publishing and editing Tanka around the globe, including 2 collections of his own and winning and placing in international and local Tanka awards, David has made a much-loved return to writing free verse poetry. He has won and placed in many free verse competitions and has had his poetry published in several anthologies."

Eric Keizer lives in northern Illinois, USA. He earned his BA in English from Drake University in 1993, and his M. Ed. from Aurora University in 2014. He has published two solo poetry collections and has contributed to three anthologies.

Miriam Ruff is a biologist, writer, editor, and poet working in Silver Spring M.D. She studied classical form poetry for nearly 2 years while a member of the Rising Moon Poetry Facebook group and discovered a wonderful world of new and interesting ways to manipulate words. Her poems and stories have been published in a variety of journals, anthologies, and websites.

Cathy McCormick is a poet from the Washington Area of the United States She has written poetry since she was a girl and now classifies herself as eccentric lady who writes poetry!

David DB Hall David is a storyteller, who weaves real life into natural scenes. He was country boy almost failing a hated English class and became a man discovering an outlet through poetry and ended up becoming an author as a challenge from his daughter. Wherever the step on the journey leads, David seeks to continue learning and sharing what he has learned.

David Bray is a Master Mariner, Nautical Historian, a painter, ship modeller and sometime poet who lives in the United Kingdom.

Laurie Grove (real name John Bowen) has been writing poetry for over 40 years

He lives in London, U.K., and for over 30 years worked as social worker. He has B.A in English Lit, and an M.Sc. in Systemic Psychotherapy. He is as yet unpublished, but hopes to bring out a collection of works in the near future.

Kevin J Ryan is an American Poet for whom I have no bio.

Yahya A. Gimba is an up and coming poet from Nigeria he has been one of my students for a year and he has gained a great grasp of poetic principles.

Oluwakayode Twaio (Teazhy) Is a young Nigerian Poet who lived as a street child for several years. Unable to go to school he looked at lessons through the classroom window. He is passionate about poetry and has a dream to produce a book of poetry about the plight of Street Children.

Christopher Buckley is an American poet who works across several genres and writes great classical poet

About the Author

Samantha Beardon is a poet and author from the United Kingdom. She has a published novel and a first collection of poetry **Caught in Passion**; the second collection will be released shortly. She also has poems and flash fiction published in several on-line publications and several anthologies including the **Rhetoric Askew** anthologies.

Samantha has been extending her knowledge of poetry by taking further courses such as those run by the Poetry School in London, plus a mentoring course and a poetry course with the University of East Anglia. Keen to share this knowledge she has been working as a poetry mentor and tutor and runs a Facebook poetry group **Rising Moon poetry** which is a small learning and critique group. Samantha has been working with several Facebook groups doing ad hoc teaching and judging. She works as an administrator for several poetry groups. Samantha is also doing poetry teaching in two messenger virtual classrooms. She is a nurse by profession and is a qualified nurse teacher with a master's degree in nursing and a degree in education.

Hideaway by Samantha Beardon

Oh, guardian of the moon - blessed one

Overcome the night to bloom

Make the world gold, dispel gloom

Hide lovers, twixt long shadows - while they swoon

Frenzied doom - as Eros arrows

strike their hearts. Their world narrows

Work your magic to protect - loves sweet glow

Do you show, beauty perfect

Or frail nature, awed, abject.

The hideaway down the hill. - my retreat

So hard to beat the views spill

Sky and sea, night and day thrill

Poetry is an Art Form therefore there is the involvement of two people the poet and the reader or listener if the poetry is performed.

I hope at the end of this book you understand there is much more to writing a poem than the outpourings of a muse onto paper. Poetry written well is a skilled craft.

Poets do not just write, they think, plan, select the best words, the best form for their message, poets utilise the musicality of language to its fullest extent. Poets may to a certain degree feel they are writing a monologue, gifting their words their ideas to humanity. Whilst there is no direct connection between poet and reader the message and therefore the poem must be viable as a means of communication otherwise it is destined to fall into oblivion.

If you write for an audience utilise your skills wisely, experiment enjoy the journey but ensure that your words are singing to an audience wowing them with their magnificence. Make your words sing!

Printed in Great Britain
by Amazon

66713026R00227